Fit For Purpose?

- the church dealing with child sexual abuse.

William J Patterson

Published by

PO Box 143, Coleraine, Co. Londonderry, Northern Ireland BT52 9AR

This First Edition Published 2009 by Family Spectrum Limited Publications

The right of William J Patterson to be identified as the author of this work has been asserted by him in accordance with the Copyright, Designs and Patents Act 1988.

ISBN 978-0-9564348-0-7

All rights reserved. No part of this publication may be reproduced, stored in or introduced into a retrival system, or transmitted, in any form, orby any means (electronic, mechanical, photocopying, recording or otherwise) without the prior written permission of the publisher. Any person who does any unauthorised act in relation to this publication may be liable to criminal prosecution and civil claims for damages.

Published by Family Spectrum Limited Publications
PO Box 143 Coleraine Northern Ireland BT52 9AR

Phototypeset by
Tate Graphics Killaloo Londonderry Northern Ireland BT47 3ST

Printed and bound in Great Britain by the
MPG Books Group, Bodmin and Kings Lynn

This book is sold subject to the conditions that it shall not, by way of trade or otherwise, be lent, re-sold, hired out, or otherwise circulated without the publisher's prior consent in any form of binding or cover other than that in which it is published and without a similar condition including this condition being imposed on the subsequent purchaser.

All quotations are from the Revised Standard Version unless otherwise stated.

List of Contents

Introduction		vii

Section One - The Phenomenon of Child Sexual Abuse

Chapter 1	The Phenomenon of Child Sexual Abuse	1
	Culture and Child Sexual Abuse	2
	Child Sexual Abuse and the Bible	3
	Child Sexual Abuse and the Church	6

Section Two - Understanding the Parties Involved - A Biblical Case Study

	Illustration:- David's Family Tree	12
Chapter 2	The Perpetrator	13
	Amnon the Perpetrator	13
Chapter 3	The Entangled	21
	Jonadab the Accomplice	21
	Absalom the Avenger	23
	David the Avoider	29
	Why Did God Allow it to Happen?	32
Chapter 4	The Victim	35
	Tamar the Victim	35

Section Three - Child Sexual Abuse and the Gospel

Chapter 5	Two Spiritual Models of Masculinity, and our Cultural Confusion	43
	The Enemy's Purpose	43
	God's Purpose - The Elijah Task	44
	The Castigating of Maleness	46
Chapter 6	The Cross and the Perpetrator	51
Chapter 7	The Cross and the Entangled	55
Chapter 8	The Cross and the Victim	59
	The Heart of God	59
	Christ Abused for Us	60
	Lack of Self Worth	62
	Forgiveness	63
	The Context of Forgiveness	66
	Forgiving God	69
	Forgiving Self	70
	Shame	71
	The Leaving, Cleaving, One Flesh Process in the Aftermath of Abuse	72
	Saving Your Life, or Losing Your Life?	76

Section Four - Child Sexual Abuse and the Local Church

Chapter 9	Fit for Purpose and Ready to Respond	81
	Authority	84
	Confidentiality and Discipline	87
Chapter 10	Restoration of an Offender	95
	Am I My Brother's Keeper?	100
	Summary and Conclusion	104
Appendix i	The Legal Position in UK Jurisdictions	107
Appendix ii	About CCPAS and Family Spectrum Limited	115

Acknowledgements

To try to acknowledge everyone who has influenced the creation of this book would be impossible. There are many authors who have contributed to my understanding of the subject matter, though the intention here is not to write an academic treatise. There are very many families with whom I have had the privilege to work over the more than thirty years I spent in Causeway Health and Social Services Trust in various posts in the Family and Childcare programme. With my colleagues we often wrestled to provide best protection for many children, and ways ahead for their families wherever possible. There is nothing like learning in the field. Many adults have, over the years, come to share their stories with Hazel and myself, seeking relief from the internal secrets and burdens that they have carried. I am very aware that learning and insight comes to us at a cost for many other people. Thank you to all those whose stories, in part, are mentioned in what follows.

The idea of producing a book was first encouraged by Barney Coombes in a conversation in late 2006. The initial plan was to produce a booklet for the Salt and Light "Roots and Shoots" series for church leaders. The material became much too long for this, hence the suggestion to publish a full-length book. I am very grateful to Mike Beaument, Douglas Mark, Brian Taylor, Bill Stone and Nuala Workman who variously proofread the manuscript from a theological, textual and professional perspective. I have incorporated almost all of their suggestions and the outcome is much the richer and more balanced as a result, though the final presentation, flaws and all, is my own responsibility. I hope that it will provoke more consideration and in the end better understanding of the difficulties.

My directors at Family Spectrum, John Matthews, Brian Taylor and Alison Mark have consistently supported and encouraged me in this endeavour, and in all the other tasks that we undertake - thank you so much. Jean Gibson and Nick Parry of Care for the Family were helpful in guiding a novice to the eventual pathway for publication, Bob Tate was invaluable in producing the final layout and design and David and Pauline Pearson of CCPAS have been really encouraging in promoting the project to final publication. I am also very grateful to Simon Bass of CCPAS for the appendix on the current legal position in the UK jurisdictions. In fact so many people have had a share in the final format and content that it has truly been a team effort, and for that I am profoundly grateful.

In the midst of a busy life it was not easy to find the time to write. In the end the time was created when I had to clear my diary for over six weeks following my mother's stroke in December 2006. As a family we spent many hours sitting with her in turns, but, for me, the times at home were poured into the initial draft of the book. This was a distraction in many ways at a time when I did not really want to be involved with many people. My mum, Maisie Patterson, passed away at the end of January 2007 leaving us with a sense of fruitfulness both from the time spent with her and that spent on the manuscript. I want to dedicate this book to her.

My wife, Hazel, and I have worked together with the many people whose experiences lie behind this book, and the cover is from one of her paintings. She has been very supportive throughout, and has faithfully kept the "tea and bickies" coming, as we say. To her and our children, a massive 'thank-you' also.

Introduction

During the summer of 1960 or 1961 my parents, brother and myself went camping to a well-known seaside resort in Northern Ireland. Jim (10) and I (12) got involved in a children's seaside mission run by a team of volunteers. On the last evening we had a sausage sizzle, bonfire and epilogue. It was the culmination of a week when we had heard the Gospel for the first time in a challenging way. I responded at the end of the talk and there beside the bonfire was spoken to and prayed with by the leader of the team. This response lasted for about another week after we returned home, but strangely, from that time, I was not able to take the Lord's name in vain without feeling deeply uncomfortable, and so I rarely did. Through most of my teenage years I turned very much against any sort of Christian faith, calling myself an atheist, arguing against while going through the outward motions of going to church with my family, as that was the only way to get the car on Saturday nights! On 1st September 1968 I eventually yielded to the Lord and came to faith in Christ one month before going up to university at Coleraine, where we still live.

The next year the Christian Union was hit by the controversy of the Charismatic Renewal in Ireland, and many tensions were caused by the debate. I was part of a group of students who went to a new house fellowship many miles away led by a man who had been an ordained minister in a major denomination, but who now was the leader of this small Charismatic community. We went for a number of weekends, and there I was introduced to the person of the Holy Spirit as one who empowered his people. I graduated in 1971 and after a year studying with a pastor in Brussels, completed my professional social work training in 1973. By the early nineties I had had five years front line social work experience, followed by five years as a team leader, and nearly ten years as an Assistant Principal Social Worker. One of my main functions in the APSW post was to chair Child Protection Case Conferences.

I remember the day when two pieces of information, which I had carried separately for some months, came together in my mind, in the light of what I was doing most days. Both the leader of the beach mission and the house group leader had been convicted of a substantial number of child sex offences. These men had no connection with each other and lived many miles apart, but both were sent to prison for the sexual abuse of children. How could it be that two men with ministries that were touching many people could have been guilty of such serious crimes?

I spent many days pondering the implications of this, as neither had made any inappropriate approach to me, but I had been within their sphere, and it seemed to have an uneasy internal connection with my work. Since then I have been involved, inside and outside work, in some aspect of almost thirty cases where a Christian leader has abused a child, only three of which have not been child sexual abuse. This does not include many more cases involving members of a congregation, some who sought help after their offences, and some who were already part of a congregation when the offences were committed. In most cases the leadership responsible for the church congregation, or the denomination, has struggled to understand and to manage the fallout of the cases. No theological or pastoral training had addressed this issue for them, and the situation has not changed much in recent years. And it is also clear that, because most leaders deal with few cases, the development of perspective and expertise is not easy for them. It is to try to bridge this gap, and to give a Biblical and practical perspective to church leaders, that this book has been written. We have a considerable journey to travel together to face all the issues.

In Section 1, we will look, firstly, at the phenomenon of child sexual abuse in culture, especially our own, then at how it is presented to us in the Bible, and, finally, at how the issues arise in the context of a local church. In Section 2 we will examine the relationship dynamics between the main parties involved when abuse takes place - the perpetrator, the victim, and those entangled with either the perpetrator or victim through family or friendship ties. This involves a Biblical case study. In Section 3 we consider the richness with which the Gospel applies to the offender, to those entangled, and especially to those who have been abused, each with his/her own set of issues. Finally, in Section 4, we consider how the local church can be fit for purpose, and ready to respond to the full range and complexity of issues that child sexual abuse will raise in the local congregation, including the management of an offender in that context.

For simplicity and ease of style, we have usually referred to the perpetrator as 'he', and the victim as 'she'. We recognise that boys can be victims of child sexual abuse, and that adult females can abuse, though only in a very small percentage of cases compared to males. To make this point repeatedly whenever the issue arises would be tedious.

SECTION ONE

THE PHENOMENON

OF

CHILD SEXUAL ABUSE

Chapter One

The Phenomenon of Child Sexual Abuse

The phenomenon of child sexual abuse has existed for a very long time; however the defining of this range of activities as 'child sexual abuse' is relatively recent. In the UK, child sexual abuse became a public issue in 1984. At the time I was working as a Senior Social Worker in a local Social Services Child Care team, and the impact of the publicity and the definition of the issue was immediately evident in our workload. In 1983 we had two referrals of child sexual abuse. In 1984 we had fifty-seven. Public awareness, and what is now the acceptability of reporting, has led to a continuing flow of cases coming to light. The taboo against telling has, since that date, largely been broken as far as this society is concerned. This does not mean that there are no pressures placed on children to keep quiet, or that it is easy for a child to speak out, but it does mean that the balance has tilted and there are now systems in place, an awareness of the duty to report, an understanding of the trauma experienced by victims of abuse, and a willingness to seek help that was unusual until that point.

The hiddenness of the issue meant that most people were oblivious to the fact that there was a problem. Those that did know did so through personal experience. However, without the vocabulary to describe that experience, or the sense of permission to speak out and find others with the same experience, it would have seemed that they were on their own with an unbelievable and unspeakable secret. In 1991 I went to Russia for the first time. My host, a psychologist, assured me that only rare cases of the sexual abuse of children had occurred in his society. However he updated me in 1994 because some work by American researchers in a town south of Moscow had discovered that similar levels of abuse were being reported there as in the West, with similar patterns of behaviour, secrecy and reluctance to believe. It only required someone to give definition to the issue and ask the relevant questions to find that many had carried a secret story that they needed to tell.

It is often asked whether the sexual abuse of children is an increasing or reducing phenomenon in our culture. It is difficult to be totally sure, as there can be no direct comparisons with earlier periods of time when no formal research was done. It is also likely that the incidence of abuse fluctuates over time in response to large-scale events such as war (many men away from home, but then, perhaps, tending to be more abusive when they return), and large-scale currents in public opinion (pubs were closed because of lack of demand during the Evangelical Awakening through the ministry of the Wesleys, and this could well have had a beneficial impact on the incidence of abuse at the time). It may be that the responses in our society over the last twenty years and more have curbed the number of cases, or have reduced the number of separate incidents in a given case before reporting. It may also be true that new avenues to proliferate abuse have been created, such as increased travel to exotic destinations where children are more available, and, more obviously, the

The Phenomenon of Child Sexual Abuse

advent of Internet related child sexual abuse. New technology has created new types of offences and has posed new challenges to the agencies that try to protect children. It is certain, however, that there has always been sexual abuse of children, and the problem is unlikely to disappear easily. Rather we will be faced with an on-going major task in developing our responses to detect and prevent abuse and to help those who have been abused or have offended.

Culture and Child Sexual Abuse

It is also asked whether our present society is worse than other cultures or eras of history in this regard? And, if so, what makes the difference? There are a number of issues buried in this question. Different cultures have defined certain acts differently (for example, whether sex with a step-child is a sexual assault or incest), and age limits such as the age of consent are different in different countries. In Germany, the Netherlands, Switzerland and Portugal in 2007, it was 16 years; in France, Sweden and Denmark it was 15 years, and in Spain 12 years. In the UK there has been variation, Northern Ireland having until 2008 the limit as 17 years, while in the rest of the UK it was 16. This was then standardised at 16 years of age across the UK, so clearly the legal limits can vary over time. Penalties vary from culture to culture for similar offences, and this can be a major consideration in responding to the issue in different settings. For example the death penalty can be given in Uganda in cases of incest. This may, in some cases, make it more difficult for family members to report sexual abuse within the family.

It has been argued that sexual abuse, mostly attributable to male offenders, flows naturally and inevitably out of the idea of male authority or domination, and that systems of belief and role definition which underpin such authority or patriarchy (such as in Christianity and Judaism) themselves predispose to abuse for this reason. I do not hold to this view for several reasons, some of which will be developed later. The main reason however is because it is historically inaccurate.

Sander J Breiner (1990) in his book "The Slaughter of the Innocents" compares five ancient cultures in their attitudes to family, women and children. These cultures are Greece, Rome, Egypt, China and the Hebrew culture. He says, *"Three features characterise cultures and families where there is no child abuse. They have (1) stable marriages, (2) marital and family love, and (3) family and marital co-operation - that is, men, women and children work together for the good of the family unit. The first and third items are characteristic of the ancient cultures of the Hebrews and the Chinese. The second quality, marital and family love, existed, but was not as extensive as the stability and co-operation in a family unit. In general we find more parental tenderness in the early Egyptian, Chinese and Hebrew cultures…. There was less abuse of children in the history of China than in most other societies. China had more family and society continuity. It had also much less separation of mother and child, and much less encouragement and support of aggression as a way of solving problems. In addition it*

The Phenomenon of Child Sexual Abuse

significantly encouraged a close father/son relationship. It stressed the importance of mothers as care givers, and it stressed the importance of education… It is also true that the Hebrews, despite their small numbers, and despite their gross dispersion into the wider Diaspora, maintained (even more than the Chinese) a continuity, a cohesiveness, a family togetherness and, obviously, much less child abuse than any other segment of society in history".[1] Breiner makes clear that at times of social disruption and war, in the Hebrew culture, child abuse increased, but that the basic family and societal structures, in the main, protected families and children. This was much less true when Israel apostasised and took on the mores of the nations around it, for which God had judged those nations. Then sexual abuse in the family, and child sacrifice occurred, and Israel came under the same judgements from God (see Lev. 18 and Ezek. 16.20-21).

Western culture has been shaped by two main cultural forces:- firstly, though decreasingly, by Christianity, and secondly by Humanism flowing from the Enlightenment. The prevailing world-view now owes much to secular Humanism, which had its origins in the philosophy of ancient Greece. Greece, of the five cultures that Breiner compared, *"was among the worst offenders toward women and children".*[2] Western Christianity generally has become more coloured and moulded by its secular culture, and less and less patterned by the Judeo-Christian mind-set that it should have, and by the scriptures that it says it believes. This would, for me, explain the fact that the church is not immune from child sexual abuse, and that it has historically been reluctant to deal with its offenders openly, positively and redemptively, with priority being given to the protection of the child, and the helping of those wounded by abuse. Where the church is a true living community that values people, and especially children, as it should, there is opportunity to put in place an understanding and practice of 'family' that demonstrates how child abuse can be prevented and repaired, and that embodies the scriptures that are given to enable us to know how to live.

Child Sexual Abuse and the Bible

The activities that we now designate child abuse are not so described in either the Old or New Testaments. It would be a mistake, however, to interpret this as meaning that the Bible does not address the issues we now call child abuse. The Bible addresses the issues, but it does so within the context of understanding that it gives for the existence and current condition of mankind. Man is a being created by God and in His image (Gen. 1.27), with all the potential for creativity and exploration with which that endues him. He was created to relate to the physical world, the creatures with which he shares the planet, and especially to his own kind within the context of family. He is given the responsibility of procreation, a working with the Creator in a way that engages his God-given sexuality and, while he walks with his Creator, his life is in harmony with the world in general and his partner in particular.

The Phenomenon of Child Sexual Abuse

Adam rebels, not out of deception as did Eve but as a deliberate act of disobedience. The Fall, as this is called, taints and undermines every aspect of his life, the first and most significant area of which was human sexuality. The couple knew that they were naked and used their own means to cover themselves and to hide from God, each other and from themselves (Gen. 3.7,8). God's temporal judgement on their disobedience, which, in part, touches the very balance of the future relationship between the couple (Gen. 3.16-19), is in addition to the immediate and automatic consequences of their sin, including the impact of the Fall on their sexuality.

The history that develops through the book of Genesis shows how this outworks in the realm of human sexuality, and the varied directions in which fallen human sexuality turns. Lamech, a descendant of Cain, committed bigamy, the first of many (Gen. 4.19; see also 26.34). Ham uncovers his father's nakedness and brings judgement on his son as a result (Gen. 9.21-27). Abraham marries his half-sister, Sarah, (Gen.20.12); Nahor, Abraham's brother, marries Milcah, the daughter of his other brother Haran, that is his niece (Gen. 11.29); and Lot has children by both of his daughters after the death of his wife (Gen. 19.30-38). These three incidences occur in the same extended family, which suggests that such familial intermarriage was accepted in the Chaldean culture from which they came.

Abraham, at his wife's suggestion, sleeps with her servant as a concubine (Gen.16.1-4), a practice that is followed by his grandson, Jacob, who has two wives and two concubines (Gen. 21-30; 22.1-13). Abraham, to save his own skin, allows Sarah to be taken into the harem of Pharaoh, in disregard of her integrity and God's promise (Gen. 12.11-20), a step again copied, this time by his son, Isaac, in the land of the Philistines (Gen. 26.7-11). The men of Sodom seek to have homosexual group sex by force with Lot's visitors in contravention of the duty of hospitality usually shown (Gen. 19.4-7). Lot's willingness to sacrifice the virginity of his own daughters to protect the men reveals something very twisted in his understanding of his responsibilities as a father (Gen. 19.8-9). Jacob's daughter, Dinah, is raped by Shechem, the son of Hamor the Hivite (Gen. 34.2) with devastating consequences, which show how seriously rape was seen. Reuben sleeps with his father's concubine (Gen.35.22) and looses his birthright as a result (Gen. 49.3-4). Judah, after the death of his wife, goes to a prostitute, as he thinks, only to realise later that it was his thwarted daughter-in-law (Gen. 38.13-18). Potiphar's wife seeks, unsuccessfully, to entangle Joseph in adultery, and then blames him for her sin (Gen.39.7-18). These are only the incidents recorded in the book of Genesis!

In a relatively short period of history fallen humanity has teased out many ways of subverting the creation order for the expression of the gift of sex. What was good when given has been warped in a variety of ways. Later we find two specific cases that illustrate the key features of what would now be called child sexual abuse ('child' in our context legally defined as being up to the age of 17 in the UK, and 18 in Northern Ireland); the rape of Tamar by her half-brother, Amnon (2 Sam.13),

The Phenomenon of Child Sexual Abuse

and the sexploitation of Salome, daughter of Herodias, and step-daughter of Herod, through her sexualised dance for a crowd of powerful men, well intoxicated at Herod's party.[3] Even in the New Testament church there was need to deal with a sex offender, although his victim was an adult (1 Cor. 5; 2 Cor. 2 and 7, especially 7.12), but how much more if the victim were to be a child, of which more later.

It may be objected that these passages do not deal with child sexual abuse as such, and that in their own culture the behaviour was acceptable, or at least not legislated against. This is a complex issue as degrees of consanguinity for sexual relations, age of consent, definitions of and consequences for sexual sin, and many other issues do vary between cultures. This is especially so between ancient cultures at an early stage of development where codified law is not nearly as extensive as in 'sophisticated' modern technological cultures like our own. However the relationship dynamics, when explored, are very up to date and typical of what experienced practioners still see in child sexual abuse cases. Surely it is amazing that an event that took place and was recorded in approximately 1000BC resonates so powerfully with contemporary studies and understanding. This is far more significant than the fact that it occurred in a different era, and cultural and legal context to our own.

Further it is not being argued that the Biblical examples used cover all the possible variations and range of abusive behaviours - no case example ever does. But, the patterns of behaviour and interactions in the Biblical examples are true to life and to many of the common themes found in cases of abuse and sexual assault. There is an overlap between many forms of abusive sexual behaviour and a Biblical approach will seek to use the material as it is and to think from there into our own culture's particular way of seeing the issues. This is as valid an approach as developing a Biblical approach to issues not specifically, or perhaps unclearly, mentioned (such as abortion), or where very conflicting positions have been argued (such as slavery).

God has mercy on men and works out his plan of salvation through history and through many cultures and, as we will see, this includes provision for the forgiveness of sexual sin, and the healing of sexual hurt caused by others, through the cross of Christ. It is our task to address the aberration of human behaviour we call child sexual abuse, in our social setting, in the light of the Biblical material, taking account of the differences of culture as best we can. When we do so, as in any area of truth, we find that there is a richness of insight that guides our thinking and how we might respond. My hope is that approaching this issue of child sexual abuse from a Biblical perspective will enable Christian leaders (for whom the book is primarily written) to think afresh about these very difficult situations and how the Word of God applies. I trust that the outcomes will be an increased ability to value and to act protectively towards the children in our congregations and society, to pastor those adults who were abused as children, and who struggle as a result, and to so manage individuals who would pose a risk to children that they find brothers who will help keep them, without, in the process, compromising any who are vulnerable.

The Phenomenon of Child Sexual Abuse
Child Sexual Abuse in the Church

We had just completed a seminar on the topic of child sexual abuse in a church training session for would be pastoral carers, when we were approached by Margaret, a lady in her sixties. She was troubled by a situation in which she was trying to help a young woman, Wendy, in her early twenties who had been sexually abused by her father. The young woman had seemed to make considerable progress, and had become strong enough to decide to move from her home and start employment a substantial distance away. Wendy had, that week, come to see Margaret in great distress. Her father had died and she had come home to attend his funeral. Margaret had expected that the event of her father's death would in some way bring a sense of release and safety at home that Wendy had never known before. Wendy had become a Christian through the process of dealing with her experience of being abused, but now was talking as if she was about to throw away her faith. She told Margaret that her crisis had been triggered by a conversation with an aunt, who was also a Christian, and who had informed her that her father had come to faith on his deathbed several days before he had passed away. The immediate crisis for Wendy was that she could not contemplate going to heaven herself if her father was already there. Her unresolved issues with him were heightened by her new faith.

This situation underlined for us again the depth and complexity of the repercussions of child sexual abuse in the life of someone who is a victim. It also made clear that there could be specific problems for a Christian who had been abused that may not arise for a person with no faith that included an afterlife. The crisis hinged on the expectation that Wendy would have to cope with the presence of her father in heaven for eternity. It is possible to be critical and say that her dilemma was based on a wrong understanding of God and how he works in the lives of people, but then many of our crises contain that element of misunderstanding the ways or the dealings of God. It is possible to be critical and say that this event revealed that she was not healed at all, and no doubt there is some truth in that, but who of us is so totally healed that we cannot be phased by some strange twist of circumstances? It is also possible to see this situation as one brought about by the providence of God, to give opportunity for Wendy's understanding of the character of God to be enhanced, and her experience of healing to be deepened.

In the situation where such a dilemma is presented, we have found that our reaction is usually to send up a silent cry for help and wisdom, while retaining a sense of composure for the sake of the person who has raised the issue! What God gave us in this case was for Margaret, and hopefully it was helpful to Wendy if and when it was passed on. We said to Margaret that only God himself knew the genuineness of the conversion experience of Wendy's father, but that it had to be either genuine or false. If it were false, God would not be conned, and would deal with the outward shallow response for what it was actually worth, just as he would deal with every

The Phenomenon of Child Sexual Abuse

sin in this man's life. If it were genuine, then God would have seen that a real work of repentance had been wrought in the man's heart. There had been no opportunity for him to make any restitution to Wendy because he was confined to a hospital bed, and she was a considerable distance away, but genuine repentance would result in true confession and reparation by the offender whether here or in eternity. God would not settle for anything short of the real thing, so Wendy could believe in a faithful God who would never allow her to be under the pressure of an unrepentant abuser for eternity. The integrity of God is the key to understanding how he might be working in such a situation. God has to help Wendy by showing her that her degree of distrust in 'father' cannot be the measure of her degree of trust in 'Father'. Her father's character is not God's character, and God will never be mocked by pretence. On the other hand, Satan, who incites and then uses abusive experiences to mar the lives of children, would win a double victory if he could provoke her to reject her faith. We do not know how Wendy responded to the reframing of her dilemma, but Margaret was clearly reassured that there could be a way to comfort her friend.

A congregation is a bigger social unit than a family, with its own networks and sub-groups. When abuse occurs in a congregation, there is potential for many people who have a sense of common identity to be affected. No two instances of sexual abuse appear in a congregation in the same way. Every instance, however, will have the same key parties involved, whether or not they all are part of the fellowship. There is always the perpetrator, then the victim, and then those who are entangled in the situation through family or friendship ties with either the perpetrator or the victim. One, two or many of the people in the congregation may thus be affected by revelations of abuse. The information may become public by an event such as the arrest of an alleged offender, or the private disclosure by a child to a youth leader of something that the child wants to remain secret. It can emerge second hand, for example where a child passes on information given by a young friend, thus involving two families in the investigation. Concerns can also be caused by the sexualised behaviour of a child, without anything specific being alleged.

The way in which the information emerges puts pressure on the first person in the fellowship who knows, and who has to decide what to do about it. It is also likely to impact on the leader or leaders who have important decisions to make about the involvement of statutory agencies, the dissemination of information within the congregation, and the management of the parties in the congregation, including the possible discipline of the offender if an offence is admitted or proved. Arrangements will be needed to maintain the equilibrium of the fellowship until the police investigation and any court proceedings are completed. Not all investigations end with a clear outcome, and the most difficult situation is where the victim continues to maintain the allegation, the alleged perpetrator continues to deny it, and the investigation is inconclusive.

The Phenomenon of Child Sexual Abuse

Children may have been abused outside the sphere of the congregation completely but come to the Sunday School. They may move with their family to a new church to put space between them and the abuser, or may be placed in foster care with a church member. Some children may be abused during church activities, or by an adult or young person, who also is part of the congregation. There may be, in the congregation, adults who were themselves abused as children. This may arise as an issue pastorally when the individual seeks help. This can happen suddenly, for example, when a news item or an investigation into a family in the church precipitates the adult into making a disclosure that they would rather have kept secret. Family or friends of a victim or of a perpetrator may seek support and help within the church, or may indeed just talk in an open way about the crisis that has impinged on their life. The incident of abuse may happen on the other side of the world, but if a grandmother is in the fellowship, she may need a lot of support and care here.

The awareness of an offender coming into the congregation creates many issues for both leaders and members. Parents will be anxious about their children. Leaders will want to know whether the matter has been dealt with by the police and courts on the one hand, and by any previous church attended on the other. Rumours and partial facts may circulate and can often fog the issues. Everyone will know what the leaders ought to do, and immediately - except the leaders who have to make many difficult and complex decisions! All of this is magnified if the offender is already part of the fellowship, and especially if the alleged victim is also part of the church. Congregations tend to split according to what information members hold, and which of the parties they know best, or believe. Family and friends of the victim tend to talk out of deep upset and in the most definite terms, while those around the perpetrator tend to hear and pass on his explanations, excuses, interpretations, minimisations and denials, even though they may have some doubts. Everyone has to deal with conflicting thoughts and feelings, and with shock, belief and disbelief. If the alleged offender is a leader the issues and the ramifications are again multiplied.

How can we start to disentangle this sort of mess in the church? That is the purpose behind this book. It is written in the belief that we can have a thorough understanding of this sort of offending from the Word of God, that we have a revelation that will guide us as we seek to help the victim, the perpetrator and those entangled by what has happened to people in their lives. We believe that the Gospel speaks to the heart of the key issues for each of the parties involved, and that the congregation is the best context to see maximum healing and restoration for the parties, provided it is prepared to take the path least travelled, through facing all the issues and working through discipleship to the word of God, wherever that leads. If a congregation embraces the challenge of addressing the issue of child sexual abuse, it will grow in many areas related to family life, and will find that it is being equipped to deal with whatever may subsequently arise. But first we need to understand the nature of the

The Phenomenon of Child Sexual Abuse

problem, and in particular the type of relationship dynamics that arise between the perpetrator, victim and those entangled by friendship or family ties with the two main parties.

Notes.
1.   Breiner, Sander, J., "Slaughter of the Innocents", Plenum Press, New York and London, 1990, p252, 256.
2.   ibid. p193
3.   Some readers may find it difficult seeing Tamar and Salome as examples of 'child' sexual abuse and sexploitation respectively, so the following argument may be necessary for some. Tamar was a virgin and clearly saw herself as at an age for marriage (2 Sam. 13.13). This means that she was post pubertal, at least thirteen years by reasonable estimate. David died at the age of 70, having reigned over Israel for 40 years - seven and a half years at Hebron and 33 years at Jerusalem (5.4-5). Amnon, his oldest child, was born at Hebron, as was Absalom, the third of six sons born there. The first mention of daughters being born to David is in Jerusalem (5.13), and Tamar is classed last along with those born in Jerusalem (1 Chron.3.1-9). Tamar was Absalom's younger full sister and half sister to Amnon (2 Sam. 13.4 - Amnon clearly perceives a closer relationship between Absalom and Tamar than between himself and Tamar). David was about 37 when he started to reign in Jerusalem, where he reigned for 33 years until his death. Amnon must have been 5 or 6 years of age by the time they came to Jerusalem. Given the family born to David in Jerusalem, which included Tamar (1 Chron.3.5-9), the age difference between Amnon and Tamar could have been anything from 7 to 11 years or more. This difference in age, and the difference in status and power between Amnon and Tamar, is what would define the rape of Tamar, a young woman in her early to mid teens, as the equivalent of child sexual abuse in our culture.

There are, in the text, a number of time-lapse statements after the rape of Tamar that help fix the time span from the end of David's reign. The murder of Amnon takes place two full years after the rape of Tamar (2 Sam. 13.23); Absalom is in Geshur for three years (13.38); he lives two full years in Jerusalem before seeing his father again (14.28); after four more years - some versions say forty, but that could not be accurate as David only lived for thirty three years in Jerusalem - Absalom's plot matures; the length of the rebellion and aftermath is unspecified (chapters fifteen to twenty); after David's reinstatement to the throne there occurs a three year famine (21.1)); and near the end of his life he provokes the Lord by numbering the people, a process taking almost ten months (24.8). The specified periods total almost fifteen years, not counting the unspecified periods, so the rape of Tamar occurred no later than the eighteenth year of David's reign in Jerusalem. Tamar was unlikely to have been born the day after David arrived in Jerusalem - it seems she was conceived there, and after the other children born there (1 Chron. 3.1-9), and the unspecified periods after the rape of Tamar could have lasted several years. We conclude therefore that a reasonable estimate of her age was thirteen to fifteen years, Amnon being at least seven to eleven years older.

The fact that it may have been culturally acceptable for her to be married at this early age does not make it any less abusive, and inside our legal frame of reference she would still have been designated a child. An example of modern day culturally legitimated marriage of a child to a much older man, that is in every way abusive, is the account of Mariam, a fifteen year old in Afghanistan, in Khaled Hosseini's "A Thousand Splendid Suns", Bloomsbury, 2007, chapter 7. We could also point to the Old Testament references to the culturally acceptable practice of child sacrifice in the nations surrounding Israel (e.g. Psalm 106.34-39), which at times Israel took on. Today the practice of female circumcision is culturally acceptable, even mandatory, in some nations (see Waris Diri, Desert Flower, Harper Collins, 1999), but is rightly seen as physical abuse in the UK.

With respect to Salome, it is not possible to be sure what age she was at the time of John's death. She is single, so unlikely to be far advanced, and it is clear that she was dominated and controlled by a mother who cared only for her own ends. Herodias was willing to let her daughter be involved in the erotic dancing in the first place, and used her as her tool in manipulation to secure John's execution. This abusing of a young woman's sexuality to manoeuvre and manipulate men, we would now see as sexploitation.

SECTION TWO

**UNDERSTANDING
THE PARTIES INVOLVED**

A BIBLICAL CASE STUDY

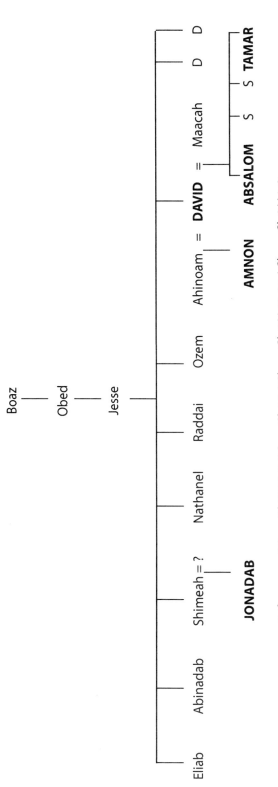

Chapter Two

The Perpetrator

Every offence starts in the mind of the offender. How this grows, and what conditions have to be achieved before an incident of abuse is perpetrated is our first consideration. When an incident of abuse occurs thought has become action, and a man becomes a perpetrator. At the same instant a child becomes a victim. The two designations are symbiotic - each implies the other. Life is never the same again for either party. Many people know the perpetrator or the child, and often some will know both. Although they know nothing of the abuse, they are already entangled in a situation not of their choosing. Their reactions will flow only when they become aware that there is an issue, whether through suspicions aroused or because of allegations made. Every instance of abuse has these parties involved and each party will have a very different perspective on what has happened. To see this more clearly we will consider a Biblical example of what would now be seen as child sexual abuse within the family - the case of Amnon and Tamar in 2 Samuel 13. However, the main character **not** mentioned in the story is God, and that raises the massive question of how we understand his non-intervention to protect the child. We have to examine the story from each angle identified above to understand the dynamics of sexual abuse, to enable us react positively rather than being overwhelmed when we are entangled.

Amnon the Perpetrator

Amnon was David's first born (2 Sam 3.2-5), and he was born in Hebron. *"David was thirty years old when he became king, and he reigned forty years. At Hebron he reigned over Judah seven years and six months, and in Jerusalem he reigned over all Israel and Judah thirty three years".* (5.3-5). The first mention of daughters being born to him is in 5.13, by which time he is already living in Jerusalem. Tamar, Amnon's half-sister, who will become his victim, is the younger full sister of Absalom (13.1). Absalom was the third son born to David in Hebron (3.3). At the time of the incident recorded in chapter 13, Amnon must have been between 20 and 24 years of age. Tamar was clearly post-pubertal but significantly younger, that is in her early to mid teens (as argued at p9 above). She was still an unmarried virgin. The age difference was therefore at least five years and maybe as much as eleven. There was also a considerable difference in status. Amnon was the eldest son and, in the normal course of events, the one to inherit the throne. He was the Crown Prince of Israel and so had a place of prominence in the household and in the nation. The fact that the abuse of Tamar would occur in the royal family of Israel should alert us to the reality that no section of society is immune from the possibility of sexual abuse. It may even be that the sense of power that comes from social position gives a sense of impunity and untouchability. Certainly the risk of exposure with its consequences does not seem in the end to have deterred Amnon.

Understanding the Parties Involved - A Biblical Case Study

Amnon goes through several stages as he moves towards the abuse of his sister. Each is important, as he could have been diverted had he made different choices, or heeded different influences. The first stage we know least about, and is the period during which he develops an obsessive desire for Tamar.

"Now Amnon, David's son, had a beautiful sister, whose name was Tamar; and after a time Amnon, David's son, loved her. And Amnon was so tormented that he made himself ill because of his sister Tamar; for she was a virgin, and it seemed impossible to Amnon to do anything to her. But Amnon had a friend, whose name was Jonadab, the son of Shimeah, David's brother; and Jonadab was a very crafty man. And he said to him, 'O son of the king, why are you so haggard morning after morning? Will you not tell me?' Amnon said to him. 'I love Tamar, my brother Absalom's sister'"(13.1-4).

Tamar is beautiful, and Amnon is attracted to her. It is likely that she came to Amnon's attention in a whole new way as she moved from childhood to being a young woman. While his noticing her attractiveness is understandable, the allowing of himself to let this attraction change into desire, knowing that she was his sister, contravened both social convention and taboos, and the Jewish law (Lev. 18.9). At this stage he does not approach her, but in his mind he becomes more and more focused on her to the point that he is *"so tormented that he made himself ill"* (2 Sam. 13.2). The difficulty for Amnon was that he wanted her but did not see any way that he could have her. *"It seemed impossible to Amnon to do anything to her"* (13.2). He obviously felt pressures from without and within not to go that way, but he had a strong and growing obsession which, at the same time, was pressing him towards her. His intent was to do something **to** her; not for her or with her but **to** her. What he wanted to do we do not know in detail but it was clearly sexual, and he was already thinking about this a lot, going over and over what he desired in his mind.

The impact on Amnon was observable to his cousin, and presumably to everyone who had eyes to see. It was seen in his face and demeanour every morning. Being *"haggard"* (13.4 - RSV, NIV) speaks of lack of sleep, and over a considerable period. It is not that he did not go to bed; he went but he did not sleep. He must have lain in the warmth of his bed, alone, awake, in the dark, recycling the thoughts and images in his mind about Tamar, and what he wanted to do to her. Becoming aroused and stimulating himself for pleasure, while mentally rehearsing his fantasy, would have been the natural outcome, again and again, each night, and night after night. The indulging of a fantasy, which would be both illegal and morally wrong if enacted, is dangerous activity. He has not yet harmed Tamar, but he is doing the internal preparatory groundwork, and as time goes on he will refine and develop the fantasy to greater heights and delights. None of this considers Tamar's wishes or preferences; it is solely about what he wants to do to her. No one knows how many men indulge in this sort of illicit fantasy life, though the extent of the accessing of pornography in our society suggests that it is common. The first stage to becoming a perpetrator has been embraced, albeit with the knowledge that it is wrong and

Understanding the Parties Involved - A Biblical Case Study

should not be acted on.

The second stage for Amnon is to move beyond the internal restraints that hold him back. In fact for a time, these forces make Amnon's fantasy seem impossible for him to achieve. However, Jonadab's input creates a new dynamic for Amnon in several ways.

Jonadab said to him, "Lie down on your bed, and pretend to be ill; and when your father comes to see you, say to him, 'Let my sister Tamar come and give me bread to eat, and prepare the food in my sight, that I may see it, and eat from her hand." So Amnon lay down, and pretended to be ill; and when the king came to see him, Amnon said to the king, "Pray let my sister Tamar come and make a couple of cakes in my sight, that I may eat from her hand." (13.5-6)

What Jonadab does **not** say is significant. He does nothing to rebuke Amnon, or to deter him from his mental journey so far. Indeed his contribution is to help Amnon over his internal blocks, and to suggest how he might get around the external hurdles, to make possible the actions that are already in Amnon's heart. Jonadab gives Amnon the embryo of a plan to help him proceed. This has three main effects on Amnon.

Firstly it gives him a sense of permission to proceed by implicitly affirming his desires, and thereby helps to reduce the restraining influence of conscience in holding him back. This overcoming of internal restraint, that is, of conscience, is a step that all would-be perpetrators must achieve if they are to proceed. External affirmation and permission either verbally, or through pornography, often has this effect in that it can be reasoned that others do it so it must be OK. Secondly, by introducing the idea of a plan, Jonadab gives Amnon the sense that it is actually possible to bring about the circumstances in which his fantasy can occur. What was previously impossible now becomes possible in Amnon's mind. This alone would increase his excitement and intensity. It may be difficult for us, and especially for victims, to realise that sexual abuse is planned, but the reality is that it is so. In some cases, especially for young offenders, it is possible that there is a much higher opportunistic element in the **first** incident of abuse, but that will not be the case in subsequent incidents, because the perpetrator knows what he has already done, and what he needs to do to repeat. This was Amnon's first offence and it was well planned, so we cannot argue for an opportunistic element in every case. Fantasy shifts to intentionality and actuality by planning.

The third effect on Amnon is to introduce the idea of pretence, the deception of others. This is called 'grooming', and is the process by which innocent people are drawn into the plan in such a way that they provide access to the intended victim. Amnon conceives and acts out a lie, and his father, who is the only one, apparently, who could authorise the arrangement, is completely taken in. The pretence includes

Understanding the Parties Involved - A Biblical Case Study

a disguise, that is a role played by the perpetrator to give a context and meaning to the contact with the victim, which deceives both the family and the victim herself. Becoming a 'patient' gives the excuse for a 'nurse' to be called without suspicions being raised.

In achieving access to Tamar, Amnon has successfully moved to the third stage in the process. He has created, for the first time, opportunity to do what he has long desired, and has now become internally ready to do. A man may desire a child, and have completed the internal work that allows him the freedom to proceed, but, until he finds the way to gain access to the child, the incident of abuse cannot happen.

"Then David sent home to Tamar, saying, 'Go to your brother Amnon's house, and prepare food for him.' So Tamar went to her brother Amnon's house, where he was lying down. And she took dough, and kneaded it, and made cakes in his sight, and baked the cakes. And she took the pan and emptied it out before him, but he refused to eat. And Amnon said, 'Send out every one from me.' So every one went out from him. Then Amnon said to Tamar, 'Bring the food into the chamber, that I may eat from your hand.' And Tamar took the cakes she had made, and brought them into the chamber to Amnon her brother" (13.7-10).

Opportunity is more than access. There is a period, while Tamar cooks the meal, during which Amnon has access to her without opportunity to do anything but watch her. He is still impeded by the presence of others in the room, even though they are unaware of his intentions. Opportunity is achieved when contact is contrived when the victim is **alone.** Risk of being seen constitutes an external restraint, and means that the presence of one or more protective adults can be enough to prevent incidents, even though every one is oblivious to the risk that is there. The seeking and finding of a role that legitimates contact with the potential victim is part of the process that ends in abuse. It does not matter whether this is a real role, such as teacher or youth worker, or a contrived one as in the case of Amnon, the intent is to gain access and opportunity. At last Amnon has his goal almost within his grasp.

But there is a final hurdle to overcome, the reaction of the victim when the real situation becomes clear. How the intended victim will react in the incident is unpredictable. Some will be more easily intimidated than others. Some will be more susceptible to inducements than others. Some, perhaps depending on age and/or awareness, will have greater understanding of what is happening than others. It is unlikely that the perpetrator will know in advance exactly how a new victim will respond. So in addition to acting out his desires, he will have to manage the responses of the victim once it is clear to her what is going to happen. *"But when she brought them (the cakes) near him to eat, he took hold of her, and said to her, 'Come, lie with me, my sister.' She answered him, 'No, my brother, do not force me; for such a thing is not done in Israel; do not do this wanton folly...............'. But he*

Understanding the Parties Involved - A Biblical Case Study

would not listen to her; and being stronger than she, he forced her, and lay with her" (13.11-12,14).

The perpetrator shows that his attitude is to take, rather than to give or to share. Amnon has rehearsed his fantasy while lying watching Tamar cook the meal. It is fresh in his mind, and now the moment comes, and he reaches for her; only to find that she resists once his intent is revealed to her. This resistance was, almost certainly, not part of his fantasy. He immediately has two options, either to stop in view of her resistance, or to continue and impose his desire on her by overcoming her resistance. Amnon uses his physical superiority to do the latter. This means not listening to her. After all, relationship was not what he had in mind.

The incident does not take long, perhaps a couple of minutes at most, but certainly nothing in comparison to the long build up. The preparation time was nonetheless necessary if he was ever to go this far. The brevity of the incident is also nothing compared to the length of the aftermath as the implications of the assault unfold in widening circles over years. The perpetrator has become what he was in intent for some time, and the child has become a victim. But the perpetrator's journey does not stop there.

What is it about the experience of abusing that so changes Amnon's attitude to Tamar, from an intensity of desire, which was prepared to take by force, to hatred and rejection? "Then Amnon hated her with very great hatred; so that the hatred with which he hated her was greater than the love with which he had loved her. And Amnon said to her, 'Arise, be gone.' But she said to him, 'No, my brother; for this wrong in sending me away is greater than the other which you did to me.' But he would not listen to her. He called the young man who served him and said, 'Put this woman out of my presence, and bolt the door after her'.………So his servant put her out and bolted the door after her" (13.15-18).

From Amnon's perspective Tamar-in-the-real-experience has not responded as did the fantasy Tamar-in-his-mind. How could she? She was totally unaware of what was in his mind, even if she had been inclined to co-operate. The fantasy and the experience will always diverge from each other, because in the fantasy the other person responds to fulfil the desire of the perpetrator, almost as an extension of him, but in reality she is a different person with her own feelings and desires. If her feelings and wishes are brutally over-ridden, how can she even begin to understand and appreciate what he wants and feels? In the end, the perpetrator is involved more in an expression of power rather than sexual feeling, no matter how he construes it in his mind. Tamar has completely failed to act as he had pictured it and so the failure is on her side, as he sees it, so she is rejected. The negative reaction is stronger than the desire in the first place. His anger is projected onto her and she is punished for falling short. I wonder whether this disparity between fantasy and the real event is the reason for the degree of physical abuse suffered

Understanding the Parties Involved - A Biblical Case Study

by some victims of sexual attack; in any case, the greater the lust before the event, the greater the rejection after.

There is a wider principle here about the consequences of unleashed sexual desire. Potiphar's wife repeatedly pursued Joseph (Gen 39), but he refused her again and again, seeking to avoid any contact beyond the necessary. When he refused her most daring advance she turned on him, blaming the incident on him and having him thrown into prison - rejection out of feeling rejected. Really she is blaming him for the disappointment of her fantasy. And, in 2 Samuel 13 also, the perpetrator, Amnon, communicates the blame to the victim, Tamar, and rejects the victim to the extent of doing her harm. Lust will always lead to rejection, and relationships based primarily on lust will always tend to be unstable and short-lived.

Rejecting Tamar and putting her out is Amnon's way of pushing responsibility away from himself. Bolting the door is his way of trying to ensure that the issue does not come back to speak to him. He is adopting a stance of disengagement from the victim and from any responsibility he has towards her. This mechanism of 'bolting the door' is to protect ourselves from come-back, and can, at least metaphorically, happen at any stage in the process. I wonder how many men have not made the full journey to becoming a perpetrator, but who have 'locked doors' in their heads about things that they have thought or done in the past. They do not want to face these people or experiences, or see them reappearing in their lives to haunt them in the future. For Amnon this is an unplanned action, not part of his original fantasy, but it expresses the fallenness of his nature in what seems to be an automatic response. The blaming of the other and the avoidance of personal responsibility are general and common marks of our sinful nature. It should not surprise us that the same reactions follow sexual sin.

From Amnon's perspective all now goes quiet. He gets on with his life, and seems to think that everything is back to normal. We are not told whether the same desire or a similar one starts to rebuild in him, pushing him to repeat the cycle he has been through. For many it does repeat and nothing helpful is learnt from the process. As far as this story goes, Amnon's crisis is over. Little does he suspect that what he has buried in his head is, for others, very much alive and still working in them. What was the end of a process for Amnon was the beginning for Tamar and others involved in their lives. Amnon does not count on the impact of his actions on his victim or on those entangled. It is also interesting that the critical stages that Amnon goes through on his journey to offending are those identified as typical of all sexual abuse cases as proposed by David Finkelhor (1979)[1], who was one of the first serious researchers of child sexual abuse in the 1960s. The stages he identifies are: the development of sexual desire towards a child, the overcoming of internal inhibitions (conscience, fear of being caught), the overcoming of external inhibitions (grooming of family and victim to gain access), and the overcoming of the victim's resistance. The end of the process is often transitory guilt and denial or

Understanding the Parties Involved - A Biblical Case Study

minimisation of the offence. After a period of quiescence the cycle usually reinstates itself, unless some sort of intervention interrupts it.

Notes.
1. Finkelhor, D, "Sexually Victimised Children", New York, Free Press, 1979.

Chapter Three

The Entangled

Many people are entangled in this episode, both within and outside the family. Some are not mentioned and some are mentioned only briefly. We will consider the three most significant participants in the story, but we need to mention all the others. They include Ahinoam (Amnon's mother), Maacah (the mother of Tamar and Absalom), many other extended family members, the maternal grandparents of Tamar and Absalom (to whom Absalom flees two years later after killing Amnon, (13.37 cf 3.3), the servants in Amnon's house (all sent out, - 3.9), especially the young man who served Amnon (13.17-18), Absalom's servants (13.28-29) and, as time goes past, many others. The most important of those directly involved in this story are Jonadab, Absalom and David, and we will consider in turn the role adopted by each. We will also briefly look at where God was as the events unroll.

Jonadab, The Accomplice

Jonadab was a first cousin of Amnon and Absalom, being the son of Shimeah, David's brother. David was the youngest of eight brothers, and the one chosen by God through the ministry of Samuel. Shimeah (called Shammah in 1 Samuel 16) appears to have been the third brother, passed over (1 Samuel 16.6-13) because the Lord looked on the heart of each of them and found what he was looking for in David. How did that experience affect Shimeah? Shimeah also went with his two older brothers, Eliab, the first born, and Abinadab to the battle in which David killed Goliath (1 Samuel 17.13), and, even if he were not present, it is not too difficult to imagine that he would have heard about Eliab's annoyance with David at David's questions about the war and the rewards for the man who could kill Goliath. He also saw David do what the many soldiers and older men were afraid to tackle. It is likely that Jonadab would have grown up hearing Shimeah's version of events. How much were his stories tinged with jealousy, on the one hand, and admiration on the other?

Jonadab is described as Amnon's friend (13.3). He had grown up with Amnon and he had cultivated a position of closeness to the future (as was thought) king. He is also called *"a very crafty man,"* (RSV - compare with "shrewd" in the NIV and NASB, and "subtle" in the KJV and RV) though why or how he had earned this description we are not told, unless it was as a result of his involvement in this instance. It would depict him as cunning, self-interested, contriving, wheeling and dealing, one using his social position to his own advantage.

The idea that he was Amnon's friend is not borne out by what he did, but he put himself forward as a friend to Amnon and, no doubt, Amnon saw him as such. Certainly Jonadab was in Amnon's confidence to a sufficient degree to probe him

Understanding the Parties Involved - A Biblical Case Study

about the reasons behind how he looked in the mornings. He saw Amnon was not getting sleep and wanted to find out what was bothering him. He was not just inquisitive, he was able to communicate to Amnon such a sense of confidentiality and trust that Amnon told him about his desire for his half-sister, who was also Jonadab's cousin. It is no small thing to convey enough confidence to another to free him to share about his incestuous desires! If you are not sure of this, try to be the sort of person to whom others can reveal such issues and see how successful you are. He would have made an excellent social worker or counsellor! Amnon trusts him sufficiently to open his heart in the most vulnerable area of his life, that of his sexuality.

Jonadab could and should have diverted Amnon from what was in his desires. He could have confronted him about the foolishness of what he was thinking. He could have pointed out that what he wanted was illegal. He could have threatened to report this to David, or to warn Tamar. He could have acted in some way to dissuade Amnon from thinking of, let alone going in, this direction. But he did nothing of this sort. Why not? It seems that he must have had some questionable purpose in his own mind, because he implicitly affirms Amnon's desires; and he puts thoughts into Amnon's head which had not been there before, suggesting a pathway to getting contact with Tamar. It will involve deception, but Jonadab is comfortable with that. He even foresees that David will visit Amnon, and has a strategy to use this to further the plan. He, at no time, shows any feeling for Tamar or her best interests. His whole focus and orientation is around the one who will become the perpetrator. He presumably knows Tamar, but he is primarily entangled through his relationship with the perpetrator.

Having sown the seed idea in Amnon's mind, Jonadab fades from the picture. He is not involved in approaching David for permission to put Tamar in place as a carer for Amnon. He cannot be linked back to whatever transpires by anyone other than Amnon, and if anything does go wrong, it will sound very weak if Amnon tries to put the blame on him. After all he did not tell Amnon to rape Tamar; he only gave a suggestion as to how Amnon might instigate some contact. In other words he has left himself with an avenue of escape - a very crafty man!

But did he foresee what Amnon would do? If he did, his actions would be even more reprehensible. And what could his possible motive be? Would Amnon's fall from grace bring him one step nearer to the throne? I think that this is unlikely as there were many other sons of David with a greater claim, and Solomon, the favourite, has already been born. Even the Lord loved Solomon from his infancy (2 Sam. 12.24-25). David at some point promised Bathsheba that her son, Solomon, would sit on the throne, as she argues and David affirms later (1 Kings 1.13,29-30). And David did this because the Lord had spoken to him about Solomon before he was born, giving his name and promising him the throne (1 Chron. 22.9-10). David's intention for his succession would have been clear, yet somehow Jonadab seems to

Understanding the Parties Involved - A Biblical Case Study

place himself within the royal household close to the centre of power at key points in the story. It seems that this is where he likes to be.

Two years later Absalom kills Amnon. Rumour that all David's sons have been killed in the incident quickly gets back to Jerusalem and to David. The king believes the early report although it later proves to be exaggerated. It is Jonadab who appears at his elbow to reassure David that only Amnon is dead. (1 Samuel 13.30-33). How did Jonadab know that only Amnon was dead? How did he know that Absalom had planned revenge from the day that Tamar was raped two years earlier? Unless he had placed himself close enough to Absalom to allow Absalom to share what was in his heart against Amnon, how could he have known what no-one else present was able to say to the king? If he knew the mind of Absalom for revenge, why did he not alert the king, or warn Amnon - who had been his friend - or do something to restrain Absalom, or to subvert the murderous plot? At what point did his allegiance shift from Amnon to his enemy Absalom? What was it in Jonadab that gravitated towards another perpetrator, Absalom, and away from the next victim, Amnon, albeit that the offence this time would be murder, not rape?

Jonadab is complex, and we cannot see all his hidden motivations, but two things are clear. He can obtain deep information about the heart motivation of others by placing himself at their shoulder, yet he does nothing to dissuade or divert the perpetrator from his crime, or to warn the intended victim, who is oblivious to what is coming. Jonadab gets entangled with the perpetrator; he does not relate to victims. As such, he fills the role of accomplice before the fact. Yet he does so in such a way that he can still use the developments to his own advantage later. Maybe he is a perpetrator at heart himself, but is too afraid to do the deed himself, seeking rather some vicarious pleasure in the act, or some future benefit. Either way, his entanglement is both negative and destructive. There is no evidence that he really did benefit in the end, for he is never mentioned again.

There are those in our culture who fill the same role. They supply the ideas, the novels, the films, the photographs, and the web sites that fuel the desire of others, though they themselves do not do the worst themselves. Their goal is to profit from the sin of others. They are accomplices before the fact.

Absalom, The Avenger

Absalom was Tamar's full brother. He was some years older than his sister and lived in his own home (2 Sam.13.20). He appears in the story for the first time shortly after Tamar emerges from Amnon's quarters, distressed and dishevelled. His immediate question to her is *"Has Amnon your brother been with you?"* This intuition is absolutely correct, but where did the idea come from? Why did he jump to such a conclusion based only on what he observed? There must have been reasons within Absalom for him to say this.

Understanding the Parties Involved - A Biblical Case Study

We carry many inner impressions of and attitudes towards others, based on past experiences of them. When presented with an event like a sister weeping, clothes torn and covered in ashes, we internally reach for or jump to an explanation even before we ask what has happened. There was no reason, from Tamar's behaviour, to suspect that she had any interest sexually in Amnon, but Absalom's collected impressions regarding Amnon come together to immediately point the finger at him. He would have noticed Amnon's morning disposition as much as Jonadab had, in fact as much as everyone. He would have seen how Amnon behaved in Tamar's presence, and felt that there was some sort of issue stirring. He had not approached Amnon, as Jonadab had, partly, perhaps, because he was not a particular friend of Amnon, but partly because he carried a gut feeling that something was amiss.

It is difficult for an individual to know in advance what such feelings point to, and it is even possible to push away suspicions, which later prove correct, as being unthinkable, blaming oneself for evil thoughts about a brother. This lack of 'suspiciability' in making all the connections before abuse occurs is common, but, after the event, we realise that we had an inkling all along that something bad was going to happen. With hindsight, we can tie together specific observations and feelings that tell us that we should have seen it coming, that we should have checked out what was happening with the other person before it got to this stage. It is interesting that Jonadab, whose motivation has already been revealed as highly suspect, was more prepared to check out the situation with Amnon than was Absalom, whose motivation was only to protect his sister. Maybe what we read in the hearts of others tells us something of what is in our own hearts! We all know what it is to say, 'I should have seen that coming.' The guilt and self-recrimination at having missed the signals will feed into the things we do next.

Absalom's immediate response is towards Tamar. *"Has Amnon your brother been with you? Now hold your peace, my sister; he is your brother; do not take this to heart." So Tamar dwelt, a desolate woman, in her brother Absalom's house"* (13.20). Absalom's reaction is to reach for Tamar to protect her. He takes her to his home to live with him and is allowed to do so, it appears, by David and Maacah, her parents. Yet in his efforts to protect her he reveals some significant things about himself in what he says.

He wants to quieten and console her, yet he uses the idea that Amnon is her brother to encourage her to be at peace. He tries to downplay the impact of the abuse to Tamar, as if it was something that did not penetrate to her very heart, leaving her desolate and broken continually in his home. It is not that he sees Amnon's act as of little importance, for he decided that same day that **he** would exact revenge against his half brother (13.32). But, to him, the avenging of the wrong fills his horizon to the extent that he is not there for his sister. Yes, he is physically present, but his mind is focussed on Amnon and the planning of the revenge. This means that he is there but not there!

Understanding the Parties Involved - A Biblical Case Study

Absalom takes responsibility on himself to obtain justice for Tamar. Why? Was the same sort of jealousy that we suspected in Jonadab working in Absalom also? He was third born son, third in line for the throne by birth. He alone of all David's sons had royal ancestry on both sides of his family (3.3), but was of mixed race with it. It is clear that he later had it in him to foment a revolt against his father to usurp the throne, so what degree of embryonic rebellion was already at work in him at this time? In any case, he fills the vacuum of David's lack of action in response to what had happened to his sister.

This sense of family revenge (instead of legal process) is still strongly present in many cultures. For example, I have encountered it in Kosovo, in the Balkans, especially in more rural areas, where it is called 'hakmaria'; the sense of obligation on a family to avenge a wrong done to a family member, by inflicting a similar wrong on a member of the other family. This is seen as a matter of honour for the family, and there is still a strong social acceptance of the practice, even though it is no longer legal. In societies where there is a more developed legal system, the responsibility for measured retributive punishment rests with the state, but the feeling that someone in the family needs to take the matter into his own hands to ensure pay back can still be strong. We have seen that many times in Northern Ireland's history.

Absalom protects his sister within his incomplete understanding of her needs. He takes to himself the duty to avenge his sister, strengthened by David's failure to act. His attitude to Amnon changes, already hinting at the outcome two years later. *"But Absalom spoke to Amnon neither good nor bad; for Absalom hated Amnon, because he had forced his sister Tamar"* (2 Sam. 13.22). Revenge, and the inner sense of need for revenge, is birthed out of hatred. Hatred is destructive towards the one hated, and to the person who hates. It takes Absalom two years to work out his hatred into the finished act of murder, but he thought about it every day, just as Amnon brooded about what he wanted to do to Tamar every night. He devises a plan to make his murderous desire possible, just as Amnon did to gain access to Tamar. He persuades David to give permission for all the king's sons to come to the sheep-shearing party, and especially to authorise the attendance of Amnon, just as Amnon himself did to get David to send Tamar to his home. He unconsciously copies Amnon's inner process!

Absalom's sin is not lust, it is hatred, yet the inner process of conceiving sin, carrying it as a pregnancy, and then giving birth to the full term action that expresses the heart sin, is exactly the same (see James 1.14-15). Absalom has so focussed on the one he hates that he becomes like him in many ways of which he is unconscious. We copy what we focus on, and become like that person. When we become like what we condemn, we are rightly self-condemned and without excuse (see Rom 2.1-3). It is not that Absalom's hatred was irrational or arbitrary; in a sense it was understandable as a response to a real wrong. However, hate turns a man into the

Understanding the Parties Involved - A Biblical Case Study

likeness of the one he hates, as he must keep focusing on the causes of his hate until these are internalised and imprinted in him. In this respect, hate is like love. We become like the one we love; as we focus on the characteristics that we love in that person we internalise them and reproduce them unconsciously. That is one reason why "looking unto Jesus" (Heb 12.2) and worshipping him is so important. We are imprinted with him over time and are reformed in his likeness (Col 3.10). We start to copy him in many unconscious ways.

"Then Absalom commanded his servants, 'Mark when Amnon's heart is merry with wine, and when I say to you, "Strike Amnon", then kill him. Fear not; have I not commanded you? Be courageous and be valiant.' So the servants of Absalom did to Amnon as Absalom had commanded" (2 Sam. 13.28-29). Absalom involves his servants in his plot for revenge. He sells the idea to them on the basis that they will be being courageous and valiant. He does so because this is how he sees himself, as a hero righting a wrong, that others with the authority did not address. He is fully justified in his own mind about this action. He is aware that there will be immediate consequences for what he is going to do. That is why he planned the place of the crime well. It took place at Baal-Hazor, near Ephraim, which is about eighteen miles north of Jerusalem. This is eighteen miles towards Geshur (Syria), which is where his mother came from, and to which he has determined to flee to escape punishment. *"But Absalom fled, and went to Talmai the son of Ammihud, king of Geshur .... So Absalom fled, and went to Geshur, and was there three years"* (13.37-38). We are not told what escape route Absalom had planned for his servants. It seems that he just leaves them to face the music for themselves. Hatred blinds us to the needs and interests of others, whom we can victimise without even realising it.

The appearance of Absalom in the court of his maternal grandfather would have caused a considerable stir. Everyone knew that he was David's son, and a prince in Israel. There is no way that an event, such as his arrival, would have been seen as commonplace or insignificant. Yet there does not seem to have been any warning of his arrival. That would have been dangerous to the plot and would have risked it being exposed. So the most natural question to arise as soon as he met his maternal relatives would have been, 'What are you doing here?' How would he have answered? He could not concoct a complete fabrication of a story, as news of the murder of Amnon would soon reach Geshur. We do not know whether news of the rape of Tamar had reached Talmai. It could well have, because two years had elapsed, but we are given no indication of this. The best approach for Absalom would be to tell his version of events, the offence against his sister, the failure of David to deal with it, his duty to avenge his sister's honour, and his courage and bravery in actually bringing her justice. That would have given Talmai reasons to protect Absalom, rather than sending him home in chains. Whatever he said was convincing, for his grandfather gave him a place of refuge for as long as he wanted it. It turned out to be for three years.

Understanding the Parties Involved - A Biblical Case Study

As time passed, David longed to see Absalom (13.39), but he was caught by the fact that he was king and could not be seen to overlook the murder of Amnon. Maybe he was also caught by the fact of his own omission in Tamar's case, and in leaving the vacuum that Absalom filled. It took Joab, who was in charge of the army, to concoct a plan to bring David to the place where he was prepared to bring Absalom home (14.1-22). Yet, even then, David could not allow Absalom into his presence for a further full two years (14.28), and only did so, in the end, when Absalom brought the issue to a head (14.29-33). There are two things of note in this period which show that Absalom's heart has not softened or changed, one much more serious than the other, but both very revealing. Firstly, Absalom married while in Jerusalem, and he had three sons and a daughter. Presumably, at least four years passed before his daughter was born, unless he had more than one wife. He named his daughter Tamar (14.27), after his sister. This shows that his sister was still in his mind and heart, and that he was still trying to do something for her, though we do not know where she lived when he went to Geshur, or when he returned. At one level, this is poignant, but at another level it shows that the attitudes he has adopted are still strong and he will not let them go. In fact he is going to go further than ever before. What has been brewing in him for many years starts to emerge after his return to Jerusalem and to his father's court. The second thing is that he starts to act the prince out of the perception that he could do a better job at dispensing justice than the existing system, that is, than his father.

"After this Absalom got himself a chariot and horses, and fifty men to run before him. And Absalom used to rise early and stand beside the way of the gate; and when any man had a suit to come before the king for judgement, Absalom would call to him and say, 'See, your claims are good and right; but there is no man deputed by the king to hear you.' Absalom said moreover, 'Oh that I were judge in the land! Then every man with a suit or cause might come to me, and I would give him justice.' And whenever a man came near to do obeisance to him, he would put out his hand, and take hold of him, and kiss him. Thus Absalom did to all of Israel who came to the king for judgement; so Absalom stole the hearts of the men of Israel". (15.1-6).

Amnon's crime against Tamar had provoked Absalom to hatred. He had put himself in the place to give his own brand of justice for Tamar, in the context of David's abdication of his responsibility towards her. He presented himself, it seems likely, to his grandfather's court as the avenger of blood, and was accepted there for three years on that basis. He returned to Jerusalem with the support of Joab, and eventually was accepted back by the man he still judges to have failed - his father, David. It seems that all these attitudes in him are now being generalised to a wider field - the kingdom. He now presents himself with his entourage to impress the public. He points the finger again at his father's lack of action to ensure quick justice for complainants (15.3). In fact, by highlighting the fact that David has not delegated authority to others to deal with cases, at least in the initial stages, he infers that David is holding the reins to himself, thereby causing unnecessary delay (15.3).

Understanding the Parties Involved - A Biblical Case Study

He starts to see himself as the man for the job, and is not slow to let the people who have a complaint know it (15.4). But his brand of justice is to hear the complaint and decide the case in his own mind before the other party has a chance to state his defence (15.3). Absalom had stood beside Tamar, immediately distancing himself from Amnon, even cutting all communication with him (13.22) in a situation where the alleged perpetrator was guilty. He now adopts this stance of siding with the apparent victim/complainant, without reference to whether or not the complaints made to him are valid. There is no even-handed investigation to determine accuracy. This identification with the victim is in stark contrast to Jonadab, who stood beside the perpetrator. Absalom is primarily entangled with 'the victim', and is no more objective than Jonadab. As a result, his input is destructive rather than helpful. Those who work with victims of abuse must realise the danger of identifying with them to the point of losing balance and objectivity. This is important, whether or not the allegations eventually prove true.

The unconscious identification with the victim that Absalom unwittingly espoused will always move him towards criticism of those in authority, whose duty it is to adjudicate. Everyone who had a complaint would see Absalom as a powerful ally, and be favourably disposed towards him as a result, to the point of feeling indebted. Thus Absalom positioned himself as a man for the people and won the hearts of the people over time (15.6). Another plan emerges in the mind of Absalom; that of taking the position as king. After all, he had been acting like a king for four years (15.7). To identify uncritically with victims, and to see oneself as the avenger of wrongs, puts a man within a short step of rebelling and reaching for the throne. This is how we start to build our own kingdom, but at the heart it is rebellion.

Others are drawn into the conspiracy, notably Ahithophel, David's main advisor. David flees from the rebellion, which is fated to be short-lived. However, at the peak of his power, Absalom, following the advice and input of Ahithophel (16.20-23), sins sexually with David's concubines in a way that everyone could see what was happening. At this point he becomes as close to the character of the man he hated as at any other time. He now copies, in essence, the actual sinful behaviour of Amnon, whereas up to now he has only copied the internal process. Child sexual abuse and rape are as much, if not more, to do with power than sexual desire. Absalom also flaunts his power in ousting his father by the sexual display of taking his father's concubines at the instigation of Ahithophel. He did not do what he did simply because he took a fancy to them. We become like what we hate, even as we fight against it. The avenger becomes the perpetrator.

But Absalom does not, in the end, gain that for which he grasped. He loses himself and ultimately his own life in the process. The saddest thing is that his support for Tamar seems to have faded away somewhere in the process. Whether she went with him to Geshur, or was left in Jerusalem, we do not know, for she is not mentioned after Absalom murders Amnon. The danger of revenge is that it obscures the needs of the victim it purports to avenge, and takes on a life of its own. The Avenger becomes more and more like the one whose sin he is trying to avenge, and ends up becoming a Perpetrator himself. The person most needing help is forgotten in the process, and in the end, the Perpetrator and the Avenger share the same fate - untimely death. The final contribution of each to the world is both negative and paltry.

David, The Avoider

One of a father's worst nightmares is to discover that his eldest son has sexually interfered with his daughter, but for David to understand his dilemma (incest in his own family) he has to face the reality that the problem did not start at the point of this disclosure. What happened in his family was not ever meant to happen in any family. The first major question for David was why did he not see the crisis coming? There were signs available to all the family that all was not well. Jonadab had picked up on these, had gone to his cousin, and had been told what was in Amnon's heart, but the signals he had noticed were available for everyone. Absalom reacted, at his first meeting with Tamar after the event, out of a gut feeling that something was afoot, and he had leaped intuitively to the right explanation, but that showed that he had had some awareness of the issue all the time. Why was David so unaware that, not only did he miss what others had detected or felt, but also he failed to see the motivation behind Amnon's request to have Tamar cook for him? David is taken in by Amnon's ruse and, without questioning, responds to his son's request and sends Tamar to help. He did not intend that his daughter would be put at risk, but he had no inkling that she might be going towards risk on his instruction.

This was not the first time David had failed to see a problem coming:- *"The Lord sent Nathan to David. He came to him, and said to him, 'There were two men in a certain city, the one rich and the other poor. The rich man had very many flocks and herds; but the poor man had nothing but one little ewe lamb, which he had bought. And he brought it up, and it grew up with him and with his children; it used to eat of his morsel, and drink from his cup, and lie in his bosom, and it was like a daughter to him. Now there came a traveller to the rich man, and he was unwilling to take one of his own flock or herd to prepare for the wayfarer who had come to him, but he took the poor man's lamb, and prepared it for the man who had come to him.' Then David's anger was greatly kindled against the man; and he said to Nathan, 'As the Lord lives, the man who has done this deserves to die; and he shall restore the lamb fourfold, because he did this thing, and because he had no pity.' Nathan said to David, 'You are the man..........'"* (12.1-7).

The Lord sent Nathan to David after he had committed adultery with Bathsheba, and contrived the murder of Uriah the Hittite. The purpose of the parable was to expose David's sin to himself, because what David had done had displeased the Lord. His sin against Uriah had also included manipulation and deceit, and David had had no shame in bringing Bathsheba to his home and marrying her after the

Understanding the Parties Involved - A Biblical Case Study

mourning period for her husband was over. Why had David not seen the intent of the parable? The simple answer is that sin either blinds a man, or creates such guilt in him that he projects his guilt onto others; that is, he sees his own sin everywhere. (For example, the Pharisees were unable to withstand the question of Jesus when they wanted to stone the woman taken in the act of adultery - they had projected their own hidden guilt on to her). David was blinded by his sin, even though he knew he was wrong deep in his heart. When asked to judge the rich man in the story, he judged himself or, more accurately, he projected the blame he carried onto the rich man, and pronounced the judgement on the rich man that he unconsciously knew he himself deserved. His 'softness' later towards Amnon and then Absalom after Amnon's murder, was really an expression of his softness towards himself.

It was David who had introduced sexual sin and murder into his family, but with repercussions that he could not have anticipated at the time. The Lord's judgement from the mouth of Nathan was *"I will raise up evil against you out of your own house; and I will take your wives before your eyes, and give them to your neighbour, and he shall lie with your wives in the sight of this sun. For you did it secretly; but I will do this thing before all Israel and before the sun"* (12.11-12). Both parts of the prophetic word were fulfilled. Amnon and Absalom copied the sins of lust and murder, respectively, in David's own household, and Absalom eventually took David's concubines in a tent on a roof (which, interestingly, was where the problem started - see 16.22 and 11.2) on the advice of Ahithophel, to make himself odious in David's sight (16.21). David had opened the door to all this misery.

David was not the only man in the Biblical record to make his child vulnerable because of his sexual sin. Herod took his brother Philip's wife, and came under the criticism of John the Baptist (Mark 6.17-18). This caused John to fall foul of the venom of Herodias whom Herod had married, but her hands were, for a long time, tied. However, Salome, the daughter of Herodias and Herod's step-daughter, was used to entertain a crowd of courtiers, officers and leading men of Galilee at Herod's birthday banquet. She danced well to the approval of the well-lubricated crowd of male officials and officers. In fact she seems to have been the only female present. Herod offered her a reward, up to half his kingdom, which by its very nature seems to have been an offer made with the liberal assistance of alcohol; why else the excessive reward for a mere dance? It was unlikely to have been a performance of propriety. To please that crowd, it would have been a highly sexualised event. This was what Herod subjected his stepdaughter to, to win the support and approval of these men. The sexploitation of Salome, as it would be termed today, was a form of sexual abuse, and not less so because there does not appear to have been any physical contact. The similarity with David's sin is however clear; sexual sin through adultery in generation one, in both cases leads to sexual abuse and murder in the next generation. I think that this is an issue worthy of research. It has a common sense ring to it, in that, if the parent opens the door by sexual sin, the children are likely to go through it in one of two possible ways. The first is by choice following

Understanding the Parties Involved - A Biblical Case Study

the lead of the parent but going further into sexual sin than the parent ever did. The second is being precipitated into increased vulnerability to sexual predation as a result of the weakening of family integrity by the parents who opened the door in the first place. The first predisposes some of the children to become offenders, the second to become victims.

When David heard of all that had happened between Amnon and Tamar, *"he was very angry"* (13.21). We are not told that he did anything, either to reprimand Amnon in his role of father or as king, or to comfort and protect his daughter. He was just angry; but with whom? If with Amnon, he could have ensured that he was punished, but he did not. It is unlikely that he was angry with Tamar, though often the anger of those entangled comes out at the point of disclosure, not the point of commission, and this can leave the victim feeling blamed for what was done to her. However in this case the offence was revealed almost immediately, so it would be easier to suppose that David's anger was against Amnon, but then, why the inaction? The anger could not have been against Absalom as it was far too early for there to be any sign of his intention to kill his brother; in fact, Absalom's intention is only revealed to David after the event. David's anger was arguably against himself. He, better than anyone, knew that judgement had been pronounced against his house, and that this was the first sign that it had arrived. Being forgiven, even by God himself (12.13), does not necessarily remove the consequences of sin, and in David's case the judgement of temporal consequences was carried out.

Why did David let Absalom take on-going responsibility for Tamar? This would have been a great opportunity to repair some of the damage, or at least to attempt to do so. But David abdicates his responsibility. Could it be that, because of his sense of having brought this on his daughter, he could not face her pain? Many victims of familial sexual abuse have more difficulty forgiving the parent that failed to protect them, usually the mother, than a father figure who caused the abuse. This may be because expectations are higher that a mother will be protective, and so the disappointment is greater when this does not prove to be the case. But in this case the unprotecting parent is David, the father. It seems more likely that David opts out, at least partly, because of the different value he placed on his different children. After the death of Amnon and the flight of Absalom, the passage states: *"the spirit of the king longed to go forth to Absalom; for he was comforted about Amnon, seeing he was dead"*. Clearly Absalom was a much more loved son than Amnon, but poor Tamar does not appear to be worth a reference, as far as David's affections are concerned.

David's blindness does not leave him. Two years after the rape of Tamar, he inadvertently contributes to the death of Amnon. Again, he does not see the crisis coming, and even gives permission for Amnon and the rest of his sons to go to the fateful party. Why did he not recognise the same pattern recurring in how he was approached? Why did he not expect trouble between his two sons? He must

Understanding the Parties Involved - A Biblical Case Study

have known that they were not on speaking terms. After the event, why does David not question the inside knowledge of Jonadab about who had been killed? David seems to be paralysed by the enormity of what is happening in his family, for which he was ultimately responsible. Being honest enough to seek and find forgiveness, as expressed in his prayer in Psalm 51, would not appear to have opened the eyes of David to how the processes of sin and judgement would continue to work out in his family. Can God renew such a situation? Surely yes, but He does not always remove the temporal consequences of our actions. It is always better not to sin, than to sin and be an example of His grace, notwithstanding how wonderful that is. David is sorely grieved by the death of Amnon (13.36), but it does not sting him into appropriate action.

These issues follow King David even to his deathbed. Solomon is to succeed him on his death, which is imminent. Adonijah the son of another wife, Haggith, wants to grab the throne. He is also a very handsome man; and he was born next after Absalom (3.4). He copies his elder brother, to whom he may well have looked up, and "exalted himself, saying, *'I will be king,'* and he prepared for himself chariots and horsemen, and fifty men to run before him", **just as Absalom had done earlier** (1 Kings 1.5 cf 2 Sam 15.1). We are told that *"his father had never at any time displeased him by asking, 'Why have you done thus and so?'"* (1 Kings 1.6). It seems that David's failure as a parent was deep and in respect of most of his children. Does failure as a husband paralyse a man in his role as father also? In David's case it seems so. David is the avoider, who neither identifies with the perpetrator (as Jonadab did), nor with the victim (as Absalom did). The avoider is the person who lets things go wrong and does not take responsibility to do what he can to minimise the harm or to repair it. He sins by omission rather than by commission. The fact that David had authority as father and king to deal with the situation, and failed to do so, makes his sins of omission more grievous.

Why Did God Allow it to Happen?

There is no record of the Lord speaking throughout the whole story of what happened in David's family, from the time he sent Nathan to give a new name to the baby Solomon (12.25), until after the rebellion of Absalom has been put down and Absalom has been killed (in fact until 21.1). Why the long silence of God? Part of the reason was that David had brought his own house under the judgement of God, and in a sense God's judgement was active by allowing events to take their natural course.

But why does he not intervene to protect the innocent? This is a massive question for those who have been abused, and one for which they need answers. An anonymous response sheet received at a course I taught highlighted this dilemma for me. A woman recorded that she had been sexually abused as a child and that the Christian leader to whom she had gone for help had also abused her. He had abused her trust and used her vulnerability against her for his own ends, also abusing her sexually. When she had made allegations against this man, others told her that she had a demon, and she was not believed. She said on her sheet that she no longer believed that there was a God, *'after all, God never stopped a single rape.'* There is a sense in which that stark statement is not completely true. We do not know how often, in response to prayers for protection or otherwise, God has actively intervened to prevent the abuse of a child or a rape, but I believe that this has happened. However, it is also clear that there is another sense in which the statement is absolutely true. In every case where a child has been abused or a woman raped, God has evidently **not** intervened to prevent what has happened, because the incident has happened.

Does this mean that God is in the same place as Jonadab, knowing what was in Amnon's heart but doing nothing to prevent it? If so, what does that say about God? Or does it mean that God is like Absalom, not alert enough to detect Amnon's intention in time, but waiting the right time to bring judgement down on Amnon's head? If so, what does that say about God? Or does it mean that God is like David, unaware of what was going on under his nose, and unwilling to deal with the offender or to comfort the victim in the aftermath? If so, what does that say about God? These questions are very real for victims and those close to them, and cause great anguish to the point, for some, that they turn away from God as a result of the fact that they remain unanswered. We may say that God cannot be like Jonadab, **and** Absalom, **and** David because their respective stances are mutually exclusive, but that is likely to be of little comfort. The victim is always left with the question, 'Where was God when this happened to me?' And the obvious implication is that God's failure to intervene says something about God and his character. Further, while the passage of time can bring some distance from the event, and some degree of reconstruction in the individual's life, the questions about God do not go away. If anything, at least for some, these questions grow and even fester.

We will revisit these questions fully in Section three, when we consider how the Gospel applies to bring healing to the victim of abuse. For now, it is enough to note that the sins of one generation are visited on the next, and that there are many terrible experiences in which heaven seems to be like brass and no help comes. People have the most awful offences committed against them, yet often we are not permitted to know the end of their story. It is easier to accept the sticky end to which both Amnon and Absalom were subjected; at least they deserved what they got, but what about Tamar? But before we can address these questions fully, we need to understand the whole experience from her perspective even though we do not know how her story ended. That is the theme of the next chapter.

Chapter Four

The Victim

Tamar the Victim

For the perpetrator the abuse event is the end of an often lengthy process; for the victim, especially when there is absolutely no warning, as in Tamar's case, the same event is the start of a new process that changes her life thereafter. Tamar was a young teenager, perhaps thirteen to fifteen years of age, waking up to life as a young woman. She would have recently reached adolescence, and the world would have been opening up to her in a new way. It is clear from what she says to Amnon later (13.13) that she was old enough to be given in marriage, something that would have happened at an earlier age in her culture than in ours. She was not experienced in life though she must have met many interesting young men among her father's officers when they were meeting with David.

Tamar is oblivious to Amnon's interest in her; if she had any awareness that he was not rested in the mornings, she is unlikely to have attributed it to any interest in her. She is not thinking sexually about her half-brother, and there is no indication that she had any interest in or desire for him. Her absence of concern about her safety is reinforced by her father's request for her to cook for and serve Amnon during his illness. She seems to be ready and willing to look after him in any practical way she can.

Although she is a princess she can bake bread. She prepares the dough, kneads it and makes the cakes in Amnon's presence. This would have taken some time while she kneaded it, waited for it to rise and be knocked back, and then put into the oven to cook (13.8). The process would have taken perhaps an hour or more. Amnon is lying on a couch watching her. He is thinking about eating, but not the bread; his mental fantasy is being rerun for the last few times as he watches her going about her business busily, totally unaware of his eyes on her back. She must have been surprised when he initially refused to eat what she had gone to the trouble of cooking for him (13.9). Then he sends everyone out of the room. Still she does not realise what is in his mind. Maybe she shrugs it off as one more expression of crankiness from a brother who has been a bit cranky recently. Then Amnon says *"Bring the food into the chamber, that I may eat from your hand." And Tamar took the cakes she had made, and brought them into the chamber to Amnon her brother* (13.10). Yet still Tamar does not suspect his intentions. He has already determined how he is going to use the opportunity he has managed to manufacture, and is about to reach the point of no return. She is still focussed on trying to get her brother to eat something to help him recover. He is tense like an animal about to spring, while she is relaxed and trusting, blind to her danger. Her servant spirit has been manipulated to bring her to this point of vulnerability.

Understanding the Parties Involved - A Biblical Case Study

Amnon propositions her, as if he was expecting her to choose to give herself to him. His fantasy was likely to have included a willing rather than a resistant partner. He probably thought that she would want him as much as he wanted her. Reality strikes home for both. Tamar realises that she is about to be raped and appeals desperately to him not to do it. He suddenly realises that she does not want him sexually, and that he is going to have to force her. There is a critical point here, while Tamar tries to reason with him. She, although a number of years younger than Amnon, is immediately aware of the potential consequences for herself - shame and ostracism. She says, *"Where could I carry my shame"?* She is also immediately aware of the consequences, for Amnon, of him doing this reckless thing. He will be seen as a fool in Israel (13.13). Amnon has never, up to this point, thought of the consequences either for himself or for Tamar. He could never think beyond the conquest. His fantasy stopped at the point of ecstasy, as if he would arrive at an eternal moment.

Tamar even proposes what seems to her a possible solution. Amnon could ask the king for her in marriage. This would mean that he would take responsibility for her future. This would mean that he would publicly acknowledge his love and respect for her. It also reveals what was the desire of her heart; long term relationship with responsibility, not just a sexual flurry with no future. We are not told whether Tamar was ignorant of the Law (Lev. 20.17), as such a proposal was forbidden by the Law, or whether common practice in Israel at that time, in disregard of the Law, created in her the perception that this was a possible solution. In any case, Amnon does not listen to her; he was never after relationship or responsibility, he was pursuing a dream, an event, an experience, a notch on his gun. And being stronger than Tamar he forces her against her will. Two, perhaps three minutes later it is over, and yet it has only just begun.

Amnon has got what he wanted, but finds that it was not what he had imagined. In fact for him the reality fell far short of what he had fantasised. It is not that he did anything different from his fantasy, but Tamar did not play her part as he had dreamt. How could she have done so? Even if she had wanted to participate, which she did not, she had no idea of what was in Amnon's mind. No sexual interaction, licit or illicit, can be successful and satisfying for the parties without good communication, or the knowledge of each other that comes from years of togetherness. From Amnon's perspective, Tamar was a total failure and a profound disappointment to him. She did not live out his fantasy. No wonder his attitude swings to that of total rejection.

Tamar has just had her virginity taken from her by force. She is probably in pain; she certainly feels humiliated, over-ruled and brutalised. The inner trauma exceeds the physical discomfort, and she is horrified by what has just happened. Then she hears him tell her to get out, and the message sinks even deeper; he did not want her, he only wanted **it.** Tamar's reaction to Amnon's rejection of her is very revealing. She sees the rejection as a worse hurt than being raped. *"No, my brother; for this wrong in sending me*

Understanding the Parties Involved - A Biblical Case Study

away is greater than the other which you did to me" (13.16). To the outsider, how could anything be worse than the rape of a young teenage girl? But, to the girl herself, the rejection seemed and felt the greater of the wrongs done to her. It is important to let the victim define for him or herself what is the worst part of the experience of abuse. It is not for an outsider or a counsellor to tell the victim how she should feel or react. To impose onto the victim our own feelings of what is worst for the victim is to abuse her again. She is rejected and excluded, and left feeling that she is the one who spoiled the experience. It is her fault that it turned out messy. In this and in many other ways the perpetrator communicates to his victim that she is responsible for her own abuse, and for the aftermath. No wonder victims find it difficult to trust someone enough to be able to tell what has happened.

Amnon gets his young servant to put Tamar out and bolt the door for good measure (13.17). The servant sees that she is dishevelled, distraught, and tearful. Five minutes earlier she would have appeared to the same servant as happy, industrious and cheerful. She cannot hide the difference. Her walls have been breached and she cannot hide it. She goes, taking some cooling ashes, from the place where she had been cooking, and puts them on her head. She rips her long robe; the very dress that showed that she was a virgin (13.18). She staggers away weeping loudly, showing by her action how she feels - dirty, torn, and wounded.

The first person Tamar meets is her full brother, Absalom. As we have seen he makes an intuitive leap in interpreting his sister's distressed behaviour. At the time it must have been a relief for Tamar to be able to nod in acknowledgement that he was correct, without her having to give painful explanations. Absalom gives her a place to be safe, but he cannot restore what has been taken, even though he does his best to play the situation down for her. At least she is free from further attack. She stays with Absalom, but the hurt changes over time to a deeper sense of depression and lostness.

Amnon, who had been having trouble sleeping, probably slept soundly that night for the first time in a long time. Energy has gone out of him, and the nights of little sleep catch up with him. Tamar, on the other hand, had never before had difficulty sleeping, but now she cannot find sleep. That night she lies awake in the dark; she goes over and over the event in her mind, reliving each stage and nuance. She wonders what **she** could have done differently, that would have led to a better outcome? Should she have shouted louder, or earlier? Could she have fought harder? Why did she not see it coming? In effect, she starts by blaming herself for what she missed, for what she did not do, and, in the end, for what was done to her. Every time she goes over the incident in her mind, she remembers furthers little details, and sees new angles in what happened.

She wrestles with the possible consequences. Is she going to get pregnant? Where can

Understanding the Parties Involved - A Biblical Case Study

she get the help and medical attention she needs? But to get help she will have to again go over what happened. She cannot ask Absalom to do what she needs; he is trying to protect her but he is a man. Then she remembers the face of the servant who locked her out - his look of surprise and shock, both at her appearance and at what he had just been commanded to do. What will he have to say to the other servants and his family when he finishes tonight? She knows that he will become 'they' as the servant talks, and that 'they' will have many interpretations of what occurred. Whom will 'they' blame? What will 'they' think and say about her in the streets? She is in no more shape to defend her reputation, than she was to fend off Amnon. The whole world is too strong for her.

She recycles the memory another ten times until she realises that Amnon was not sick at all. His 'illness' was just a ruse. She then knows that it was all planned and not a spontaneous attack. She remembers him watching her while she prepared the meal for him. Did no one else see what was coming? Why did no one think to let her know she was at risk? Even her father asked her to go to Amnon to help him. Why did he do that?

Then another thought strikes her. How did Absalom know to ask her if Amnon had been with her? Could he have guessed this might happen, and, if so, why did he not warn her? Question after question comes to her in the night as she realises more and more of the process Amnon had to take to get time with her, and of the implications for her immediate and long term future. How can she ever again hold her head up? What will people be saying about her? Who will ever marry her now? What will become of her? Where are my mum and dad? Why are they not here? I feel so dirty and I need a wash. The scream after the event comes much louder than at the time. The horror solidifies into something that is always there. And where is sleep to blot it all out for a short time?

Life goes on in Absalom's house. Tamar is not the same as she was. If no one comes to see her, and gives her an opportunity to talk, it feels like another rejection. If someone does come, she wonders what is his or her real motive in talking with her. Absalom has changed too. He is moody and pensive, and though he does not say what is on his mind, it is obvious that he has cut all communication with Amnon. Amnon is just carrying on his life as if nothing has happened, in fact it seems as if most people are going about their business as if nothing did happen. Did it happen or was it a nightmare? Absalom, whether known to Tamar or not is not clear, starts to plan revenge against Amnon. This must affect the atmosphere in the home, and be hinted at by little comments let slip from time to time. Does this help Tamar heal? Or does it tend to engender further bitterness and hatred in her also? In fact, what does help her heal? There is no clear help coming towards her from what we are told in the passage. *"So Tamar dwelt a desolate woman in her brother Absalom's house"* (13.20).

Understanding the Parties Involved - A Biblical Case Study

Two full years later there is another crisis in the family when Amnon is murdered by Absalom. How did Tamar feel about that? Did she delight in the revenge taken by her brother, or did she feel that all her old wounds were reopened, as her experience became new news again? After all, Jonadab knew why Amnon had been murdered, and he was not slow in telling the king (13.32-33). It could not have been long before everyone was talking about this new twist to her story.

We do not know whether Tamar was with Absalom when he fled to Geshur. Either she was or she was left behind. If she went to Baal-hazor with Absalom, even if she was not privy to the plot, she must have had some idea that something was afoot, and if she had not been told of Absalom's intention to kill Amnon, she must have had big questions about his strenuous efforts to include him in the party. If she did know what was going to happen to Amnon, she was complicit in the plot. When she arrived in Geshur with Absalom the necessary explanations for their unexpected coming would have identified her, not as a granddaughter visiting her grandparents, but as a victim of rape and incest recently avenged and seeking asylum. That is how she would then have perceived herself, and how she would have been perceived in the minds of those she met. How could she ever get away from what happened to her?

If, on the other hand, Tamar did not go with Absalom to Geshur, she must have been left behind in Jerusalem. She would have felt abandoned by the only person who had thus far tried to protect her, and she would have had to answer the inevitable questions from the family about what she knew of the plot to kill Amnon. She may even have been seen as being complicit, whether or not she knew, for she lived in the murderer's home. No development in the life of the victim is independent from the experience of being abused; everything is interpreted inside the aftermath of abuse, and there is no escape.

Years later, after Absalom had returned to Jerusalem, he had a daughter and named her Tamar, presumably after her aunt. Tamar would probably have been in her twenties by this time. How would she understand the naming of her niece after her? Would she be pleased at Absalom's thoughtfulness, or would she have been tempted to think that he was replacing the old torn useless Tamar with a new, clean, perfect one? When would her struggles about what was done to her ever end?

We do not know the end of Tamar's story. That is not unusual, because it is not possible to define when the end comes. Is it after one year, or five, or fifty? Or is it after death, and if so how can anyone know how it turns out? Thankfully, we are not left in the Old Testament. We have the New Testament, which throws a whole new perspective on such traumatic experiences, and we need to consider how the Gospel speaks to these situations, for us in our lives if not for Tamar.

SECTION THREE

CHILD SEXUAL ABUSE

AND THE

GOSPEL

Chapter Five

Two Spiritual Perspectives on Masculinity, and how our Culture Confuses Them

Any family experiencing the horror of child sexual abuse is impacted in many ways and provoked to many responses, some of which can be as serious and devastating as the initial abuse. We have looked at David's family in some depth to illustrate this point, because we should never think that sexual abuse is a stand-alone issue. It becomes woven into the fibre of the family, and it affects and colours all the relationships involved in the ensuing history. This raises the question as to whether there is any substantial hope of putting right what has happened, and whether the Christian Gospel has anything to say to the layers of sin, hurt, retaliatory sin and on-going pain. This section is written from the conviction that not only does it have something to say, but that what it does offer is unique and substantial. That does not mean that a painful journey can be avoided, but it does mean that for the honest and the willing there can be massive healing. The Gospel speaks to the perpetrator, to those entangled and to the victim, and the further we go we shall see that we all are those who have sinned, and, to some degree, we all are those who have been hurt by being sinned against. Therefore, whether or not we are victims of sexual abuse, we all need the experience of forgiveness and healing, but each in our own specific way.

The Enemy's Purpose

The sexualisation of a child violates the trust of that child. It precipitates the child into what should be adult experience, and pushes the child towards being an adult, at least in terms of the responses that the child is induced to make. This leads to a loss of childhood, or, more exactly, a loss of 'childness'. In spiritual terms this serves to destroy, in a measure, the child's natural receptivity to the kingdom of heaven. Jesus said, *"Unless you turn and become like children, you will never enter the kingdom of heaven"* (Matt 18.3). The natural childlike direction towards simplicity, truth and openness is blunted by an adult's thirst to use the child for his own selfish purposes.

Biblically, a generalised attack on child victims has always preceded the raising up of a Deliverer. Indeed it may be the very thing that precipitates the sending forth of the Deliverer. Moses was one of the boys that Pharaoh tried to kill at birth, out of his fear of the growing strength of the slave nation serving him (Exodus 1). Many boys died but Moses was preserved. Jesus, the expected Messiah, was the target of Herod once he had ascertained where the Messiah was to be born. Many families were bereaved but Jesus escaped because Joseph was warned by an angel in a dream to go to Egypt. In both cases the attack was ruthless, causing devastation in many families, yet in the providence of God neither succeeded in achieving its main target, and, in both cases, the Deliverer, in the fullness of time, came forth and fulfilled God's call on his life.

In both cases it is not hard to see a malevolent will behind the political expediency of Pharaoh and Herod. Pharaoh, with good reason, feared the increasing numbers and strength of the Israelites, and produced his plan to cull the slaves because of this. His goal was to secure his own kingdom. Herod, an Edomite, that is a descendant of Esau, did not want the prophesied ruler of Israel, descended from Jacob, Judah and David, to displace him, and so planned to eliminate him before his life was properly underway. It is unlikely that either saw the spiritual significance of their acts, or that they were aware of what was prompting them to so oppose what God was doing. It is doubtful whether they even saw the situation in the context of God doing anything. They were taking politically expedient precautions to protect their positions, but 'the enemy' would have been aware of bigger purposes at work, even if he could not see who the Deliverer would be. The sacrifice of a few children is of no account to Satan if only he can keep his hand on the tiller of the world, as he sees it.

Today we see the attack on children in a very generalised way both through child abuse, and through abortion. Many children do not see the light of day, and many who do are subjected to interference and abuse of trust - the very quality that Jesus says opens them to the kingdom of heaven. I have been often surprised by the proportion of people who share that their abuse started just before or just after they made their first response to the Gospel. Below and beyond the motivation of the human perpetrator, there lurks here the influence of the evil one, who is profoundly bothered by something. Could it be that his dirty war is based on the same strategy of attacking the weakest, and destroying or spoiling their lives to prevent or mar the rising of a generation that will be the nearest to seeing and welcoming the return of Jesus to the earth? The evil is too profound to rule out such an idea as baseless.

God's Purpose - The Elijah Task

God has a purpose and, we believe, it will prevail to overcome the sin of man and all the plans of the evil one. He also has a strategy to bring about his purpose. It involves us, and we will call it the Elijah Task. The last two verses of the Old Testament are as follows:- *"Behold, I will send you Elijah the prophet before the great and terrible day of the Lord comes. And he will turn the hearts of fathers to their children and the hearts of children to their fathers, lest I come and smite the land with a curse"* (Mal 4.5-6). What can anyone do to stop the Lord judging a land because consecutive generations have turned away from each other at the fundamental level of the heart? It is the quality of inter-generational family life that God highlights as the key symptom that in its absence calls down, or in its presence averts, the judgement of God against that land. 'Elijah' is given the task of turning the hearts of the people from inter-generational strife to family unity to avoid the outcome that will come unless 'he' succeeds in his task.

Luke throws light on what is meant by this fearsome statement at the very end of the Old Testament. He records what the angel said to Zechariah in the temple while telling Zechariah that he would, even at his age have a son called John. *"He will turn many of the sons of Israel to the Lord their God, and he (John) will go before him (the Messiah - Jesus) in the spirit and power of Elijah, to turn the hearts of the fathers to the children, and the disobedient to the wisdom of the just, to make ready for the Lord a people prepared"* (Luke 1.16-17). John will go before the Christ to prepare the way by turning the hearts of the fathers to their children. Renewal in the nation does not happen without a renewing of family life at the very centre. Here the emphasis is not on judgement to be avoided, but on the preparation of the people, the land, for the Lord. The main thrust is to restore the hearts of fathers to their children, with society-changing, and destiny-changing consequences. This is what God wants to happen, but Elijah, or someone who goes before in the spirit and power of Elijah, is needed to prepare the way.

Why Elijah? Well this heart impregnated his entire ministry. He raised the widow's son from the dead and **delivered him to his mother,** inspiring the family to faith (1 Kings 17.24). He prays down fire on the altar with the words, *"Answer me, O Lord, answer me, that this people may know that thou, O Lord, art God,* **and that you have turned their hearts back***".* God sent Elijah to anoint a successor, and Elisha was the one he was told to anoint (19.16). He respected Elisha's desire to say farewell to his parents (19.20-21), and together they started the schools of the prophets to replace the generation of those murdered by Jezebel (18.13). Elisha's last glimpse of Elijah, as he is taken up in the chariot to heaven, draws forth his perception of his spiritual mentor, **"My father, my father"** (2 Kings 2.12). Elijah is sent by God to rebuke and pronounce judgement on Ahab, after Jezebel has manipulated the death of Naboth and seized his vineyard for her husband. Naboth saw the vineyard as *"the inheritance of my fathers"* (1 Kings 21.4). In other words, Ahab was expecting Naboth to disregard his God-given right to inherit the land from his fathers, even as Ahab himself disregarded what God had put in place for the stability of the society. Inheritance is what one generation passes on to the next because the hearts of fathers are turned towards their children. This was not just an attack on property; **it was an attack on family,** especially on fathers and sons, on society, and on the ways of God. We are told that it was not just Naboth that died, but also his sons (2 Kings 9.26), so his whole line was destroyed. No wonder Elijah was there to oppose the king. For a Jew this was serious as eternal life, in his mind, was tied into his descendants. Ahab was undermining the structure of the family and the spiritual connection across the generations.

Finally, there is the question why Elijah appeared in the first place? Elijah appears at the start of 1 Kings 17. The previous verse describes the fulfilment of a prophetic word given to Joshua son of Nun, which pronounced a curse on the man who would rebuild Jericho (1 Kings 16.34). This was fulfilled by Hiel of Bethel, and the curse that Joshua had pronounced (Josh. 6.26) was enacted by Hiel in the laying of the foundation, at the cost of Abiram his first born, and in the setting up of its gates, at the cost of Segub his youngest son. This sort of ritual sacrifice was demonic in nature, and both the sacrifice and the rebuilding of Jericho were against the clear will of God. **How much worse can a man go in turning his heart away from his children than to deliberately sacrifice them for his own advancement?**

In response God sends forth Elijah to confront the king who both allowed Hiel's actions to happen and to go unpunished. God sent Elijah to withstand the currents in his society towards paganism, and to turn the hearts of the fathers to their children, as the last attempt to avert widespread judgement on the whole nation, and to turn the people back to God. If we are to have a similar impact on our day and age, we will have to confront the same forces in our society. God's heart is for children and for family, and we minimise the importance of these things at risk of finding ourselves opposing God himself. This does not depend on having a family of our own. Neither Elijah nor John the Baptist were family men, but the thrust of their lives was to value what God valued and to pay the price for saying so.

The Castigating of Maleness

Child sexual abuse is mainly perpetrated by men. Over 95% of offenders are male, and of the small number (in comparison) that are female, a sizeable proportion are perpetrators along side, or under some duress from, men who abuse. The tragedy of the last twenty five years or so (sexual abuse became a public issue in 1984) has been that it was not the church, through its ministry to people who were hurting, that identified child sexual abuse as an evil that required massive systemic responses at many levels in our society. The issue came to the public's attention through the work of women's refuges across the nation. Erin Pizzey (1983)[1] opened the first of these in the UK in 1971, and they have multiplied since then revealing the degree of hidden domestic violence that had been occurring.

The bringing together of women who had experienced domestic violence naturally led to them sharing their stories. In time it became clear that these stories were often not just about physical violence, but also about sexual violence from partners. Further sharing revealed that the problem went even deeper. Many women had connected with men who represented to them the sort of maleness to which they were accustomed, and they realised that many had been physically and sexually abused as children. This was disturbing as it suggested that women could tend to select partners whose behaviour was similar to what they, as children, had known and come to expect from men. Not surprisingly, given the context of these emerging findings, the women concerned were not predisposed to think well of the men that had been in their lives, indeed, of men in general.

Child Sexual Abuse and the Gospel

At the extreme pole of perception, there were those who saw the sexual and physical abuse as an expression of male assumptions of dominance, which usually it was, but then, by extension, as an expression of male headship and leadership. In the end it was seen as the logical expression of any faith system that legitimated male leadership. This included Christianity which was blamed, by some, to the extent that the Bible was rewritten referring to God as 'she' to counteract the imbalance, as it was perceived. The church would do well to refrain from being over critical about this as there were a significant number of instances of abuse by those who claimed to be Christians, even leaders. Recent revelations about systemic abuse in, for example, the Catholic Church, such as the 2005 Report into sexual abuse by priests and religious between 1962 and 2002 in the diocese of Ferns in Waterford, Ireland, where twenty-one priests were named, has done much to reinforce these perceptions. Investigation subsequent to the report revealed that over 240 priests across Ireland had allegedly abused children over a similar period. This is not to lay the blame solely at the door of the celibacy issue. A very significant factor was the control of education by the Catholic Church, which would have made education in a church institution an inviting target for those with paedophile tendencies as a means of accessing children. Celibacy and its correlation with child sexual abuse may well be an issue to research, but my own experience of nearly thirty cases involving abuse by leaders of the church, has included only one that was **not** some variety of Protestant.

What do we say to these charges? Popular culture forgets two major facts as far as Christianity is concerned. The first is that Satan is, throughout the Bible, described, without exception, as male. It is not just God who is described in this way. Indeed there are a minority of passages that attribute female characteristics to God (e.g. Psalm 131 and Matt 23.37), though the majority do refer to Him in masculine terms. The 'ministry' of Satan is described as *"to steal and kill and destroy"* (John 10.10), so we are left with the Biblical reality of two very different models of Maleness. The first is typified by what we have seen attributed to the thief. He is a taker, a user, a dominator, and an abuser. The second is typified by Christ himself, who made it plain that he came to serve and lay down his life, and not to be served (Mark 10.42-45), and that those who followed him were to do likewise. The things, which cause a man to abuse a child or a woman, are, frankly, characteristics of Satan not of Christ. The fact that a man can abuse, while claiming to be a Christian, does not mean that he is so, if his life represents the other model of Maleness. This is hypocrisy and we should be the first to say that this is what it is. My question is, why does our culture not rail against the model of a male Satan, rather than, as it often does, blame his characteristics on God, who is so far from being like Satan as light is from darkness?

But why does God allow the abuse of children to happen? Why does he not intervene to prevent such crimes against the innocent? The apparent silence of God can be the most difficult aspect of such experiences, as he seems to neglect the victim and ignore the offender. The answer to this is to examine what the question is really asking. The question of why God allows the abuse of children is only one aspect of a bigger set of questions. Why does God allow war? Why does he allow terrorism? Or AIDS? Or poverty, or suicide, or divorce, or the character assassination of gossip, or lying, or cheating in a multitude of ways? The question is really why does God allow sin? And that means, why does he not intervene **immediately** to right the millions of wrongs done to so many people across the world? When put like this, the intent of the question comes to mean, why does the Final Judgement not come now? Then every hurt and offence will be dealt with, and every offender will receive his or her true desserts, unless he or she is in Christ, when we will receive **his** true desserts. The question, 'Why does God not intervene **now** to deal with those who have sinned against me?' cannot be separated from the question, 'Why does he not intervene now to deal with **my** sin against others?' It is a fearsome thing to demand the Final Judgement immediately, because where will any of us stand? We are really asking, why does God delay the final accounting of the universe?

"Do you not know that God's kindness (in deferring judgement) *is meant to lead you to repentance…For he will render to every man according to his works: to those who by patience in well-doing seek for glory and honour and immortality, he will give eternal life: but for those who are factious and do not obey the truth, but obey wickedness, there will be wrath and fury"* (Rom 2.4,6-8). The delay is opportunity. It is opportunity for the offender, all offenders, (and I am an offender too), to repent. It provides opportunity for the victim to seek and find the grace of God in the healing that he brings. It is opportunity to be changed in a process that brings with it eternal benefits, for *"this slight momentary affliction is preparing for us an eternal weight of glory beyond all comparison"* (2 Cor. 4.17). And it appears that, from God's perspective, the eternal benefits for those who believe are worth the delay. Maybe the real question is why do we doubt? Why do we delay to receive such grace? Why do we impute to God such negative motives? Why do we continue to hurt and be hurt, to resent and to blame? Why do we continue to refuse when he speaks to us, rather than to inquire what he has done for us? Maybe the real questions are to be asked of us rather than of God.

The other main fact that our culture forgets is that Jesus, The Sin-Bearer, The Saviour, The Healer, is male, and that it was as **a man** that he took on himself all our sin (our abuse of others) and all our pain (the abuse we have received), so that we might not have to carry the penalty of sin on the one hand, and that we might not have to remain unhealed on the other. The truth is that he has dealt with both our sin and our hurt on the cross, and that there is a wealth of forgiveness and healing to experience and to be changed by.

It will be said that none of the above excuses God for not intervening, because the perpetrator is an adult who should know better, and the child is surely innocent. But, maybe, from God's perspective, the perpetrator's whole life is seen at one sweep -

Child Sexual Abuse and the Gospel

the child, the adult, the old man - whereas we only see in the present. God sees what happened in the child-life of the perpetrator, and can hold his later actions within that perspective. He also sees the consequences that will flow in the victim's adult-life, and how the current experience will warp, or perhaps deepen, the adult-to-come, because of the choices she makes in response. He sees what we all do with the cards we have been dealt, and where we each get it wrong, and want to excuse ourselves because of what was done to us. Maybe, from God's eternal perspective, we have all been wounded in some way, and then have all contributed our own share of hurts to others weaker than ourselves. Maybe we all need a Saviour, who deals with what is truly our responsibility, and a Healer, who deals with the wounds we have received from the hands of others stronger than us. If we all need Jesus to forgive us and to heal us, maybe God has done more to deal with the human mess of all sorts of abuse than we give him credit for. Because the Gospel deals with these very issues it is profoundly relevant.

We now have to consider how the Gospel applies to the perpetrator, those entangled and the victim, in turn. We need to evaluate whether we have been blinded to what He has done for each, and whether there really is hope, mercy, forgiveness and healing for each of us beyond anything we have dared to think before.

Notes. 1. Pizzey, Erin, "Scream Quietly or the Neighbours Will Hear", Pelican, 1983 (republished).

Chapter Six

The Cross and The Perpetrator

The truth is that we are all perpetrators; it is just that we have each perpetrated different perpetrations! We have all perpetrated and come short of the glory of God (Rom 3.23), but we like to think of some wrongs as being greater and more evil in God's sight. We especially easily see those things perpetrated against us as worse than those done by us against others. We judge others by their deeds, but we judge ourselves by our intentions. Maybe God sees us more clearly than we see ourselves, that is, maybe we do not see ourselves accurately. But this child cannot be as guilty as the man who abuses him/her. That is true if we take a snapshot. But if the whole of life is seen together, maybe we are more like each other than we like to admit. Each generation can easily try to feel better by blaming the previous one for the difficulties we have had to contend with, and so it could go back to Adam, only to find that this is what the Bible does; it goes back to source, to Adam who was the first one to sin, and whose likeness we bear, yet in a way that does not deny the hurt done to us by others, nor the fact that we have made essentially the same choices, and have hurt others. If we are all perpetrators then we can all experience the same hope, for perpetrators who get honest, take responsibility and repent have a hope of forgiveness. Indeed there is no other way to be forgiven.

Are not sexual perpetrators, especially those who perpetrate against children, in another category? In terms of sexual sin I consider that there are three levels of seriousness: sin that is consensual with another adult, sin that is coercive and imposed on another adult, and sin that is coercive and is imposed on a child. We shall consider each in turn.

"For this is the will of God, your sanctification: that you abstain from immorality; that each one of you know how to take a wife for himself in holiness and honour, not in the passion of lust like heathen who do not know God; that no man transgress, and wrong his brother in this matter, because the Lord is an avenger in all these things, as we solemnly forewarned you. For God has not called us for uncleanness, but in holiness. Therefore whosoever disregards this, disregards not man but God, who gives his Holy Spirit to you" (1 Thess 4.3-8).

This passage deals with consensual sin between adults, and makes it very clear that it is not God's will. God expects a negative - to abstain from immorality. This means sex outside of marriage, probably before marriage, since we are to know how to enter into marriage the way God intends. This general immorality is the opposite of knowing how to prepare for and enter marriage, and is likened to how the heathen **who do not know God** behave. It is possible, though tragic, that believers behave as those who do not know God. When those who are Christians act like the surrounding society they act against God and his will. If we do so we also wrong or defraud our brother (v6). This brother is not the person with whom we might sin, but a third party who will be cheated if we are immoral. Perhaps it refers to the woman's eventual husband, from whom something is stolen, that God intended she and he would eventually share. Paul says that God is the avenger of this sort of behaviour (v6), which is strong talk to those who are supposed to be under the grace of God. To disregard this is to disregard God who gives his Holy Spirit. It is no small thing to be sexually immoral; it is not only sin against the partner and against one's own body (1 Cor.6.18), it involves disregarding God, and cheating a brother whom we may never meet. The passage is clear, that God avenges sexual sin in the life of a believer. If this is true of consensual sin between adults, how much more is it true of coercive sexual sin against a child?

The second category is coercive sin against another adult. There is an example of such a person in Corinth. He is the man who was living with his father's wife (1 Cor 5.1-13). The fact that the relationship was coercive in some way is clear because only the offending man is to be dealt with through discipline. *"Let **him** who has done this be removed from among you (v2) … … I have already pronounced judgement in the name of the Lord Jesus **on the man** who has done such a thing (v3-4) … … You are to deliver **this man** to Satan for the destruction of the flesh, that **his** spirit may be saved in the day of the Lord Jesus"* (v5).

Norman Hillyer dates the first letter to spring AD 54, and the second to a year or so later, [1] so some time has elapsed when Paul writes a second time to Corinth to exhort the church to follow through the process of dealing with this man. *"But if **any one** has caused pain, **he** has caused it not to me, but in some measure - not to put it too severely - to you all. For **such a one** this punishment by the majority is enough; so you should rather turn to forgive and comfort **him**, or **he** may be overwhelmed by excessive sorrow. So I beg you to reaffirm your love for **him**"* (2 Cor 2.5-8). The clearest statement showing that he is dealing with a perpetrator, not just a sinner, is in Chapter 7. *"So although I wrote to you, it was not on account of **the one who did the wrong**, nor on account of **the one who suffered the wrong**, but…"* (2 Cor. 7.12). He is addressing the situation of a perpetrator and a victim, not of two equally consensual sinners, and how the church should deal with the former. His sin was of a kind not even found among pagans (1 Cor 5.1), and he is not just to be rebuked but excluded from the church for a period, yet with the hope that he will repent and that his spirit may be saved. Yes, there is hope for him, but he is going to experience tough love as the means of grace. The woman concerned is either not a part of the congregation or else she is indeed an on-going member of the congregation to which the offender is eventually (we presume) restored. Whichever is the case, she is described as the one who suffered the wrong; that is, it is clear that she was the victim of some sort of abuse or coercive relationship.

What then about the person who sexually abuses a child? Is there grace for such a person? This is a tougher question than it appears. It is easy to reason that, because

Child Sexual Abuse and the Gospel

Christ calls all men everywhere to repent, there is by inference real hope, even for the paedophile. I believe that there is hope, but that the process of receiving God's grace will be tough. Many professionals, on the other hand, have little or no hope that these men can be fundamentally changed. They do not think in terms of a 'cure'. In many ways I agree with their caution, but my main question is not in terms of a 'cure' as such; it is more to do with what true repentance would look like in such a case. How does Jesus see such a person? He has a lot to say about the man who stumbles a child in Matthew 18, and this we will examine. The phrase "stumble a child" does not explicitly deal with child sexual abuse; it is used in a much wider way. However, if abusing a child sexually is not included in that which stumbles a child, I do not then know what could be included.

"Whoever receives one such child in my name receives me; but whoever causes one of these little ones who believe in me to sin, it would be better for him to have a great millstone fastened round his neck and to be drowned in the depth of the sea" (Matt 18.5-6). Our true attitude to Jesus himself is revealed by the way we treat a child. We should not be deceived; this is the basis on which Jesus evaluates us. However, millstone 'therapy' is **not** his punishment for a man who stumbles a child; it is a preferable alternative to ever abusing a child in the first place. The millstone treatment is **better**… than what? (18.6). It can only be better than causing a child to sin in the first place.

What then is the punishment due to one who stumbles a child, in Jesus eyes? He does not tell us, but proceeds to talk about self-amputation of the parts of the body that cause a man to sin. He cannot mean a literal amputation. We see very few self-amputees in the church, so we seem to agree on this. A man with one hand is just as able to abuse a child, and a man with one eye is just as able to indulge in child pornography, so literal amputation is not the issue. Yet Jesus is talking about an amputation so radical and clear-cut that he uses this vivid picture. It is a self-imposed operation. No one else can do it for us, or to us. Experience of child sex offenders does not fill anyone with confidence that many are willing for this sort of radical and publicly obvious dealing with their inclinations to stumble a child. None of this excludes the possibility of legal action against the perpetrator or efforts to help him change, but it underlines that the key to change will be his ruthlessness to deal with himself, without which no lasting change will be brought about.

The eternal stakes are high for such a man. He can cut off the offending parts of his life and *"enter life"* maimed or with one eye, or he can avoid the pain and public evidence of the necessary inner work, and be *"thrown into eternal fire"* (18.8). These are the words of Jesus. There is hope of entering life, but it cannot coexist with any failure on his part to deal with his sin at the very root. This is all made clear before there is any talk of forgiveness later in the chapter. We do not help sex offenders by fudging the issues, and trying to make it easier for them in the church than Jesus does.

Child Sexual Abuse and the Gospel

There is then provision for the offender who is entreated, but does not become honest, and so cannot be won (Matt 18.15-18). He is finally and bindingly excluded from the church. Soft talk and easy answers just will not do. God commands repentance, and there is something wrong if the church does not require the same. **But**, if your brother listens to you, at any stage in the disciplinary process, that is if he softens, sees his sin, and truly repents, then you have won your brother. Christ has atoned for his sin, but he has been won by his brothers. We will address the outworking of this process in a congregation in the last section.

There is one further distinction that needs to be made. A man, who abuses a child before he comes to faith, will gain much greater credibility by open acknowledgement of his past, than one who commits the same acts while already professing to be a Christian. The former cannot realistically come under church discipline for matters that took place before he believed; the latter desperately needs to embrace restorative discipline and accountability if he is to have any credibility at all. However both will need the same support and vigilance of friends and brothers to find a place within the fellowship that is both safe for them and for any children within the sphere of the fellowship.

It is sometimes objected that the Corinth example deals with a man who offended against an adult. This is true, and it is also true that one who offends against a child creates further more serious issues for the church than one who has offended against an adult, bad as that is. However this is an example of a young church being guided through the exercise of discipline in a difficult situation, and it therefore speaks also to our case. If such rigorous discipline is required for one who offends against an adult, how much more will it be required for one who offends against a child? The response required when a new case arises will at least involve the discipline of exclusion that is owned by the whole congregation. If we say that our response cannot include restoration to membership after true repentance has been evidenced, then we stand in a different place to Christ himself, who, if the child offender submitted himself to radical heart surgery, (and this is a big 'if') would re-include him in eternal life, and by extension in the congregation, if this is possible. It is not that we like this responsibility - to be our brother's keeper in such an extreme situation, but that we have it, whether we like it or not. To be true to the truth we can neither allow this sort of offender to be left undisciplined on the one hand, or simply rejected on the other, at least until the full process of attempted restoration has in each specific situation failed. In any case the question is not "Should we try to deal with these offenders (rather than put them out)?" It is "How must we deal with these offenders, given that they are already present in the church, whether known or not?" What needs to be done in the context of the church will be explored further in Section Four of this book.

---

1. Hillyer, N., in "The New Bible Commentary Revised", Ed. Guthrie, D., Motyer, J.A., Stibbs, A.M., and Wiseman, D.J., IVP, 1970. Others have given slightly variant time scales.

Chapter Seven

The Cross and the Entangled

In the case of Amnon and Tamar, three main characters entangled in the action (Jonadab, Absalom and David) were so in destructive ways. By this we see that not everyone reacts in the same way to abuse, and that there are various patterns of response that are each destructive. These patterns can even be opposed to each other but their impact is uniformly negative. The accomplice, the avenger and the avoider appear in many situations and none of these reactions has a redemptive input. There were other lesser characters that were equally entangled. The servants who were close to the action, perhaps the young lad who bolted the door, more than most, all had a juicy story to tell, and some of them would have become the gossips that broadcasted, relished and even embellished the story. They unwittingly create difficulty for the main players by so doing, for their actions add a public dimension that puts everyone's responses under the microscope. The public dimension has repercussions for the victim and the perpetrator in particular.

These people who are entangled, mostly independently of any choice they have made, are nonetheless responsible for their actions and reactions, and God will call them to account in due course. Our immediate reactions expose our underlying attitudes, and the fact that a reaction is both wrong and destructive shows that the underlying attitude, although hidden, was wrong all the time. Those entangled, whether they side with the alleged perpetrator or the victim, are generally distressed, and when we are in distress the real person inside usually hangs out. There is something quite parallel to the scene around the cross in all of this and, when trying to help someone struggling with sexual abuse in their circle of family and friends, we often take them to the account of the scene around the cross of Christ.

There we find a wide cross section of people and reactions. There are the soldiers who care little for the feelings of the prisoners or their families, and who do what they do as their line of work. It is how they make their money. There are the plotters and planners of the murder of Christ, clad in a cloak of religious respectability, who do not directly get their hands dirty, but who want the execution to take place more than any others. The Pharisees are in one sense the Jonadabs of the piece. Then there are the disciples, friends of the victim, but thrown into confusion and running away from the action out of fear. All their ideas have been exploded by what is unfolding, and they cannot think straight, or determine what to do. The women are there too, loyal but helpless, loving but weeping, willing to be identified with Jesus but unable to influence events.

The betrayer is there, finding that the outcome of his actions against his friend goes in a totally different direction from what he had ever expected. His 'fantasy' about what would ensue has been mugged by a gang of ugly facts. The consequences for him are serious, as he loses his place in his circle of friends, and soon takes his own life, as he cannot face what he has actually done. The crowd, fickle to the last, changeable in opinion and easily manipulated by the propaganda of the authorities through the media, still wants to be there to satisfy their voyeuristic impulses. There is nothing like a good scandal, and it provides plenty of food for gossip (see Luke 24.18). There is even the ultimate pain for the victim; his Father, who could intervene to rescue him, is silent and distant and does nothing to help. The sense of forsakenness and emptiness is profound. Where do we stand in that scene? It is important to identify this place, as it is from this place that we view the crucifixion and understand what it does to us and means for us. In the same way it is important for us to identify where we stand in relation to an abusive event in our circle of life, as that is where we must face our reactions and what they reveal of our own hearts.

The accomplice not only has to face his assistance to the offender, which renders him an accessory before the fact, but also the reality that he had not the nerve to do the deed himself. Those who collude behind the scenes but do not offend through fear of being caught ultimately share the fate of the perpetrators; in fact they are first in line (Rev 21.8)! The avenger not only has to acknowledge his hatred of the perpetrator, and the murderous heart this reveals, even to the point where he substitutes himself for God to bring down the judgement deserved, but also the horror that he has become like the one he hates through the very hating, and is therefore fully self-condemned. The avoider has to face his neglect of duty, and the hidden motives that motivated him to back off, leaving the mess for others to deal with. But he will also experience the reality that a responsibility avoided does not disappear, and that he will eventually have to face and deal with the issue. With his weakness in procrastinating, the longer he delays the more complicated, difficult and humbling it will become. And the crowd, that is we ourselves, will have to examine what in us is curious, nosey and pass-remarkable about the exposed pain of others. Why is it that we want to see, and be on the fringe, and discuss, and savour, the dirty linen of others? Abuse raises all these questions for each of us, and unless we can find a redemptive position in ourselves towards the scene, we will be part of the problem. For fallen human beings such as we are, that means a resurrected position, because we all fall short at the first exposure.

The Gospel, thankfully, is for sins of omission as much as for sins of commission. It is for the soldier who saw the victim as the Son of God in the end. It is for the women, who will be first at the tomb to see the evidence of the resurrection, and who will be in the upper room fifty days later. It is for the friends who 'chickened out', denying Jesus or running away. Next time, humbler, wiser and stronger, they will see it through. It is even for the Pharisee who comes by night, afraid to identify himself openly for fear of the social consequences, but who goes by night to pick up the broken pieces, and eventually finds his place where he should be. It is for those who were not the hands-on perpetrators, but were nonetheless perpetrators after their own sort, by what they, that is we, did and did not do. Honesty will take us to the place of heart searching. Did we sense something amiss and hold back from checking out, because of fear, because others would think we had a dirty mind, or simply through lack of love? It is not enough for those who are entangled to condemn the guilty, or to dismiss the allegations of the victim as false or malicious, if we are not prepared to be under the searchlight ourselves. When we become vulnerable ourselves, we see our own need of the grace of God, and take a step towards being part of the answer, rather than part of the problem.

Matthew 18 shows us that the entangled need to be careful about their attitude to the victim. *"See that you do not despise one of these little ones; for I tell you that in heaven their angels always behold the face of my Father who is in heaven,"* says Jesus (18.10). It is easy to blame the victim without consciously intending to do so. It was the disclosure of the victim that brought the issues to light and forced us into the discomfort of facing what had been done. Our reactions are triggered by the disclosure, not by the offence, which may have happened much earlier.

There are times when we need to be among the *"one or two others"* (Matt 18.16) who support a victim seeking resolution from the offender (18.16). And we are certainly called to be the small group that prays and sees it done, however long it might take (18.19). The Father does not will that any of these little ones should perish, and we should have the same heart. We cannot throw the Gospel at the situation or at those involved; we need to have the Gospel in us to be able to show, live and speak it in a way that deeply connects with the individuals caught up in what someone dear to them has done, or has had done to them. We are presented with an opportunity to become like Christ in how we respond, and it does not come easily. But how does Christ see and reach to the victim, so that we can start to see what we must become? That is the focus of the next chapter.

Chapter Eight

The Cross and the Victim

There are four main forms of abuse of children - physical, emotional, and sexual abuse, and neglect. There is also organised abuse, which often contains elements of the first four types of abuse, especially sexual abuse, but is distinguished by the fact that a number of adults conspire together to abuse a number of children, and to provide each other with opportunities to abuse and with alibis afterwards. The final, less recognised, form of abuse is system abuse, which occurs when the agencies that exist to protect children, by over- or under-reaction, actually harm children by their responses. It is not that this is the intention of the agency, but it is the effect. In over thirty years as a social worker, I have never met a single colleague who wanted to be on the front pages of the tabloid press. Yet there have been a number who have found themselves there. It can seem unforgivable that a child care professional acts in such a way that a child is actually harmed as a consequence, yet I have a lot of sympathy for those who must take critical decisions at a point when only partial information is available. It is possible to act to protect and then find that a child has been removed prematurely, or to under-react only to find later that the situation was more serious than the initial information to hand suggested or, worse still, to miss something that later proved to be crucial. In most exams scoring 70% is a distinction, however 70% in a childcare case may not be good enough to protect a child. This is a very complex issue and not easily disentangled. The variety of means, forms and combinations of abuse is such that no situation is simple and straightforward.

The Heart of God

Earlier we raised the question of 'Where was God while a child was being abused?' His apparent absence and non-intervention is easily interpreted as indifference at best, and as malevolence at worst. What is God's heart towards victims of abuse? In Matthew 18 they are described as *"little ones"* (18.6,10,14). The little ones are stumbled (18.6) by an adult perpetrator; we then are warned not to despise the little ones (18.10). The next section is about the shepherd who leaves the ninety-nine sheep on the hills to seek out the one sheep who strays, for *"it is not the will of my Father who is in heaven that one of* **these little ones** *should perish"* (18.14). It is one of the little ones who were stumbled that becomes the sheep, the little one, that strays. We should not be surprised that this connection is so, and we should be slow to condemn those who stray when we do not know their full story. However it is not the Father's will that such a little one should perish, and it is clear that the shepherd is out there searching for the strays, leaving, says Jesus, the rest of the flock to do so.

This version of the parable of the lost sheep is different than the version in Luke 15.

3-7. In Luke's version the sheep was fully responsible for its own lostness, because its return with the shepherd is described as *"a sinner who repents"* (Lk.15.7). In Matthew's version the little sheep that strays, and needs to be brought back, is a little one who was previously stumbled by someone more powerful and influential than itself. The balance of responsibility here is very different than in Luke's telling of the parable. There is something very sad about this little one who strays. She (or he) has been put into danger and stumbled by an adult, only to stray later, apparently of her own volition, into further danger isolated from the flock. It is as if the early experience of being stumbled has impaired the little one's capacity to perceive danger, so she becomes a risk to herself. When the Lord finds the stray, and it takes real effort on his part, he rejoices more over her than over those who were never stumbled and who never went astray. The question should be, not 'Does God care? but 'How does God care for, help, seek and find those who were abused and went astray?'

Christ Abused for Us

When we consider the passion of Christ in terms of abuse it is quickly clear that his experience embraced various forms of abuse. The physical element is obvious, whipping, punching, scourging, crucifying. In the end this was severe enough to kill him. Emotionally he was rejected, spat on, mocked, given a sham trial, separated from friends, and taunted. His human rights as such were completely by-passed. He experienced neglect through the deprivation of clothing, food, water and sleep. The agencies of religion and law, which were created to protect the weak, conspired, in the persons of Caiaphas, Pilate and Herod, to illegally bring about his downfall and death. This was both system and organised abuse. There was even a satanic element as Satan winnowed him to find a flaw, but could not do so. But what about sexual abuse; surely there was no element of that?

I was part of a team carrying out training for social workers who would be working directly with sexually abused children. One of the team, a child psychiatrist, was illustrating a point by reference to a case he had dealt with. This involved a seven or eight year old girl, who had been tied down and forcibly raped. He illustrated this by stretching out both arms sideways so that his body was in the form of a cross. I immediately saw something beyond the point he was making and it has remained vividly with me since. I realised that Jesus was pinned down on the cross, spread-eagled and restrained so that he could not protect himself, or cover himself, or even wrap his arms around himself to defend his vulnerability. He was forced open in posture and revealed to eyes and spear. He was not covered by a large loincloth as he is depicted in renaissance art; he was hung up in public, totally naked to be shamed and humiliated. He knew what it meant to be exposed without ability to change his position or hide. The motive of Jesus' killers was not sexual, but part of the impact of what they did to him was. He carried the inner experience of the victim of abuse in his sense of helplessness, exposure, shame and abandonment. For him the worst part was the sense of being forsaken by his Father, and this wrung his most anguished cry from him. *"My God, My God, Why have you forsaken me?"* (Matt 27.46). The fact that this fulfilled the prophetic word in Psalm 22.1 does not mean that the gut-wrenching experience was any the less real for him.

What happened to him was unfair; he did not deserve it in any way. It was not for things he had done that he had to go through the cross. He was unfairly on the receiving end from those who crucified him, from all of us, because he died for our sins, from Satan who vented his fury on him trying to find a weakness, and even from his Father. Yes, he had agreed with the Father that he would take this on himself for us, but that did not make it fair for him. If anyone thinks any experience in life is unfair, he should consider the unfairness of what we did to Jesus Christ in order to gain another perspective. This is God himself in the flesh, delivered to the greatest unfairness of history at the hands of a world that ganged up on him rather than yielding to him his due.

There are three levels in the abuse of a child. The first is the act perpetrated on the child. This in itself is offensive and hurtful. Secondly, there are the subtle ways in which the perpetrator speaks and acts to share or impose the responsibility for the abuse on the child who is abused. It can come subtly as an invitation - 'Come and let us play the little game that **you** like to play.' Thus the initiating motive is projected onto the victim, a subtlety that a child finds very difficult to fend off. The adult is always going to win such mind games. Or through the offer of bribes or inducements - ice cream, fishing trips, sweets etc. - the child who has become a victim is made to feel that she wanted the abuse because she wanted the inducement. This is exactly what the perpetrator wants to engender in the child, to secure the silence of the child, and to make himself feel that it is the child, not himself, who is to blame. Amnon was angry with Tamar for her failure to enact his fantasy, and punished her by eviction as a result; that is, he blamed her for the actuality of the experience falling far short of the fantasy. The third level of abuse is when the child, who has experienced the abuse, tries to tell and is not believed. The disbelief of the listener turns her story into a lie, and some malicious motive in telling 'the lie' is thereby inferred. Thankfully Tamar was believed, and victims of sexual abuse in our culture are now much more likely to be believed, as we understand more of the dynamics used by perpetrators to skew the child's perceptions. But in the past it has not always been so, and many have been rejected or vilified for telling by those who were afraid of the consequences of believing.

We find these three levels of abuse in the experience of Jesus also. Firstly, all sin is perpetrated against him as the second Person of the Godhead. Sin is not a doctrine for the Lord; it is an affront; it is an act of opposition and offence. It is done in the face of God, no matter how pleasantly it is dressed with gentle words and appealing excuses. Sin pains God deeply, and costs God deeply. It is not an intellectual matter for him, it is excruciating in the extreme. Secondly, Jesus bears the blame for the very sin done so cruelly against him. He has to pay the bill for the damage deliberately done to him. This is the second level of hurt and pain. Thirdly, many who are told laugh it off. They ridicule and disbelieve, both what they (that is, we) have done to him, and what he has done for us. I do not think we have any idea what it cost the Lord to die for us, and then have someone turn his or her back on that degree of love. There is no sin or pain that Jesus has not willingly taken on himself to open a door of hope for us in regard to what we have done, or had done to us. But he looks for a response that shows we at least partially grasp what we have done to him, and what he has done for us.

Any victims, regardless of the nature of the abuse sustained, will find the grace of God inviting them to open up to that grace. And, **if** they find God in their trouble, the worst done to them will serve only to enlarge their hearts, and increase their capacity for eternal joy. This is a big 'if'. It is the prospect of eternal joy that sustains us through pain, just as it did Jesus (Heb 12.2). But it is also the finding of God in our pain that creates the capacity in us for expanded joy in eternity, because it is only the experience of pain embracing, and being embraced by God and his grace that can enlarge our heart. Knowledge puffs up, but love builds up (1 Cor 8.1). Thus God can never be outwitted, for He can turn anything upside down and make the worst experience a doorway into a deeper experience of his grace. The trials of this life, **if** we find God in them, are already suffused with grace. However, the converse is also true, as C S Lewis[1] has pointed out. The troubles of this life, **if** we refuse the God who is seeking us in and through them, become to us the anteroom or foretaste of hell. So all is of grace, and at the same time all is of faith. No one can commit in that direction for another; each has to take a conscious step for himself, and we each will go as far towards God as we are willing. He has not left anything undone that would prevent us from going the whole way. The wonder of what Christ has done can be seen in specific instances which unlock specific hurts, as we will now consider.

Lack of Self-Worth

A common experience of many who have experienced sexual abuse is to feel worthless, valueless, or cheap. It is as if the experience communicates to them that they do not matter; what does matter is the other person's gratification. This sense of low self-esteem persists long after the actual abuse has stopped, and indeed long into adulthood. It affects every aspect of life, not just the sexual area, but the expectations that the individual holds of people and life in general.

Graham was in his forties when he came to us seeking help. He had been a rent boy between the ages of ten and fourteen. In this period he had had many bad experiences of what would have been seen as extreme forms of abuse. In situations of multiple, severe abuse we often ask whether there was one particular experience, or one type of experience, which was, for the victim, worse or more difficult to live with than any other? In this case Graham acknowledged that there was. He explained that he knew 'this thing' must have been happening, but on the occasion in question he actually saw it happen, and it had had a profound and destructive influence on his life ever since. He had been taken by his 'minder' to a client's flat. As the minder was leaving, the client gave him a ten-pound note for services that Graham would have to render. At that point Graham knew that he was worth ten pounds. This sense of being virtually worthless never left him and, long after the sexual abuse had ceased, he was still struggling with the sense of being worth only ten pounds.

An immediate request was sent to heaven for wisdom, and instantly something came to mind that seemed to connect to his experience. I said to Graham, 'I know someone who has had a very similar experience. He was a very important and well-known person, and in fact you may well know of him. In spite of who he was, he was on one occasion valued down to thirty pieces of silver.' For a brief second Graham sat puzzling until the penny dropped, and light spread across his face. There are two profound realisations in this connection. Firstly, Jesus, the Son of Glory, was devalued to a handful of coins by the one who betrayed him. This means that he knows by experience how it feels to be treated as cheap or worthless. This also is part of the burden that he has borne for us, so that we do not have to carry such a weight ourselves. We can lay it down, and let him carry the curse that this has represented to us.

Secondly, this same Jesus had put a very different value on Graham (and you and me). He had esteemed Graham, and each of us, as more valuable than his own life, in that he laid down his life for us. This creates a choice for each of us; we either believe the value put on us by people, the world and our experiences of life, or we believe the value put on us by the Son of God himself. Graham could choose to believe that he was worth only a ten-pound note, and let that cloud and grey his whole life, or he could choose to believe the value put on him by the Father and the Son, and let that renovate and colour his whole life. To be brought from a sense of being locked into a low self-evaluation, to a sense of choice, is in itself liberating, but it is a liberty to be walked in each day. We live out of our understanding of who we are. Knowing who we are in Christ, and how he perceives and values us, gives to us dignity and worth independent of any experience that has intruded into our lives. No one has to languish under a sense of low self-esteem, irrespective of where it came from. We have been given the liberty and value of becoming the sons of God.

Forgiveness

We have met many people who have been urged, by well-meaning Christians, to start by forgiving their abuser, and who have tried time after time to do so, only to feel that they fail. They continue to struggle with the aftermath of the abuse and an overlay of condemnation because they feel they cannot forgive or have not forgiven. Clearly forgiveness is important for the freeing of the abuse victim herself, but what is the problem for such a person? We have found that the root is often the counsellor's lack of understanding of the nature and dynamic of child sexual abuse, which leads to the application of the correct remedy prematurely. We saw earlier that embedded in the process of abuse is the subtle transfer of responsibility, consciously or unconsciously, from the perpetrator to the victim. The victim is spoken to and treated in such a way that she picks up the feeling that she is at least as much to blame for what happened as the adult was. This is not objectively the case, but it is what the child comes to feel and carries into adulthood. Jesus' perspective is that the adult perpetrator *"causes the child to sin"* (Matt 18.6). The child is involved in the sin, but not as the initiator, nor as the one who is liable in God's sight. If the victim carries forward a sense of guilt or responsibility for what happened, it is **not** a sense that the Lord has put on that person. It is false guilt.

Let us say that June feels she is as guilty and responsible as her grandfather for the sexual abuse she experienced at his hands when she was aged between six and eight years of age. She feels this because she was always given sweets and made to promise that she would not tell **their** secret. Her compliance with this bribery and pressure to promise leaves her with the sense of complicity. The disparity of age and status is not felt by her to place more responsibility on her grandfather. When she reaches adulthood, she effectively holds her grandfather and herself each to be 50% responsible for what happened. From this perspective she tries to repent for her 50%, and never gets relief, and she tries to forgive his 50%, without ever feeling that she has really and decisively achieved forgiveness. She has said the words, but it does not feel true. No amount of attempted mind-over-matter gymnastics changes how she feels. The root problem, in her perceived failure to either repent or forgive properly, is that she has not corrected her misunderstanding about responsibility for the abuse in the first place. She is trying to repent for her 50% of the blame, which God does not attribute to her at all. She is trying to forgive his 50%, which only goes half way to addressing the harm he did to her, and the responsibility he holds before God. She cannot succeed in either task without reallocating responsibility first. The proper reallocation of responsibility must precede effective forgiveness, and a counsellor who does not grasp this subjects the victim to further abuse, because the victim struggles to forgive in good faith but never feels she succeeds.

Claire came to see us with her fiancé. They were engaged to be married, but Claire could not bear to be touched by Gordon, even to hold his hand. Both had been married previously, and had been divorced before they had become Christians. Claire had been an alcoholic, receiving in-patient treatment to detoxify about four years earlier - around the time she came to faith. She had been in an abusive first marriage, and Gordon was the first man in her life to treat her with respect. This made her aversion to touch even more difficult to understand. Rightly, they recognised that this had to be dealt with before they could be successfully married. Claire had several children to her first marriage, the eldest of whom was a teenage girl.

Child Sexual Abuse and the Gospel

Our first session with them was like swimming through treacle. Claire acknowledged that there were difficult experiences in her past that were interfering with her present relationship, but she had not been able to share these with anyone, including Gordon. She could not really share with us while he was present, though she wanted him to be there. At the end of the session we suggested that she consider writing her story to us, as an aid to getting past her roadblock about talking. She agreed to think about this, and they left. We were not at all sure that they would be back, but later in the week we received an unsigned letter detailing her history of abuse. She had been abused sexually by her father, stepfather, grandfather, and uncles. In her first marriage she had, on many occasions, been subjected to marital rape as part of the on-going violence in the relationship. She had become an alcoholic, trying to anaesthetise her pain through alcohol, to the point that she could not keep a home together. She became part of a group of alcoholics, all men except herself, and had been 'gang-banged' more times than she could remember. The letter helped us understand why she was averse to touch, even though Gordon treated her completely differently to anything she had known before. She had been in sobriety for about four years at this time, but was finding that her new relationship with Gordon was triggering all these negative responses in her.

When they came back for the second session, Claire was very nervous about how we might see her or react to her, and could hardly admit that it was she who had sent the letter. We asked her what had been the worst experience, or type of experience, from her viewpoint, in all that she had written to us. She told us that it had been an incident with one of her uncles. We initially thought that this must have been a horrendous event in the light of all she had shared in the letter. We eventually asked what had marked out this experience as the worst because it did not seem as extreme as many of the others. She told us that this experience was worst for her because she had initiated it. She felt she was objectively responsible, notwithstanding that she had been programmed to be sexually compliant for years before this event had happened. She was willing to confess this event as sin and receive forgiveness from the Lord, and then immediately had the ability to give the rest of her hurt to him and receive his healing. She finished the evening by burning the letter as being part of her past that was now covered by his grace. It underlined to us again that our presumption as to what was the worst part of an abusive history could be far from the reality experienced by the person who had lived that history. About a year later, we met the friend who had referred Claire to us, and inquired as to how she was doing. She told us that Claire and Gordon were married and their relationship was going well. Claire had had a period of weeks on antidepressants when her teenage daughter got into some trouble, but apart from that she had been well. Distinguishing between what was her responsibility and what was not was one of the major keys to her release.

Child Sexual Abuse and the Gospel
The Context of Forgiveness

There is a further aspect of forgiveness that must be considered, and that is to do with the circumstances that exist at the time we consider forgiving an offence. There are three main contexts in which the issue of forgiveness arises, and each is different in meaning. The first is when the offender remains unrepentant, and in fact may still intend to offend further against us. The second is when the offender apologises and appears to repent, only to re-offend again, apologise again, and offend again. Transitory guilt is typical of child sex offenders, as is repeat offending. The third situation is where there is genuine repentance and the offending behaviour stops. These three alternatives each present the victim with different issues when the question of forgiveness arises.

There is also a distinction between offenders who are found out and those who voluntarily confess their wrongdoing. Those who are exposed can appear to repent and apologise, but in reality they have little choice if they are to retain any credibility. The big question is whether they would have stopped the sin if exposure had not intervened. Those who confess and bring their own sin to light elicit greater confidence from others that their repentance is heartfelt and genuine.

How should a victim manage the issue of forgiveness while the offender is still intent on offending against her? Can she actually forgive in this circumstance, if forgiving means 'pronouncing forgiveness'? There are two New Testament examples of this predicament, and they are very illuminating. The first is Stephen, who, even as people who **continue to want him dead** are stoning him, prays, *"Lord, do not hold this sin against them"* (Acts 7.60). He does not fudge the issue of responsibility; he calls what they are doing, albeit with the authority of the Sanhedrin, sin. It is wrong, and Stephen is the victim of the wrong. Neither does he say, 'I forgive you,' or speak directly to those stoning him. He does not **pronounce** forgiveness; he **prays** to the Lord that they might be forgiven. This is not a matter of splitting hairs; it is of very deep importance.

Was his prayer answered? Well we can believe that, at least in the case of the young man Saul, it was, but later not instantaneously. We do not know what became of the others who were throwing the stones. If Stephen had pronounced forgiveness, would they all have been forgiven on the basis of his heart-felt request? If so, their state of heart and quality of repentance are irrelevant! This cannot be so. If we pronounce forgiveness on someone who still holds to the sin against us, we are in danger of unwittingly making ourselves wiser than God! God has a heart that we would be forgiven, and he has gone to extreme lengths to provide a basis on which we can be forgiven, but he does not tell anyone that he is forgiven before there has been clear repentance (Acts 2.38).

There is a second example, which is even more significant; it is that of Jesus himself.

Child Sexual Abuse and the Gospel

Luke tells us that he was crucified between two criminals, and that he prayed for those who killed him, *"Father, forgive them; for they know not what they do"* (Lk. 23.34). Jesus does **not** pronounce forgiveness on those guilty for his death, he prays for them, just as Stephen would do later. The perpetrators in his case were still set in their minds, and determined to kill him; their heart had not changed in any way, so it was not possible to say 'I forgive you,' or to pronounce forgiveness; it was appropriate to pray for their forgiveness or, more accurately, to pray that they might be so convicted of their sin that they would repent and so in the end come to seek and receive forgiveness. The heart that will say, 'I forgive you,' when an offender apologises, will say 'Father, turn their heart and bring them to forgiveness,' while the offender remains stiff-necked and unrepentant. The centurion seems to have had revelation of some sort and confesses his conviction that this was the Son of God (Luke 23.47). The repentant thief is told he will be in Paradise with Jesus later that day precisely because he voices his confession and repentance (Luke 23.40-43). Most of the remaining onlookers were not softened in their hearts, and retained their guilt. Whether they repented later, we do not know.

If, to look at the issue from another angle, the prayer of Jesus had been answered by the Father, and he had immediately granted what his son had just asked, then those who were crucifying Christ would have been forgiven on a different basis than any other people in Biblical history; they would have been forgiven on the basis of Jesus' request alone, without any need for repentance and faith in Christ on their part. This again clearly cannot be, so it follows that Jesus' prayer was not answered immediately, except perhaps in the cases of the centurion and the penitent thief, and for many of those implicated, may never have been answered affirmatively at all, though some or many may have come to faith after Pentecost (the "you" and "they" in Acts 2.36-37). To pronounce forgiveness is to absolve, to intercede for forgiveness is to reveal the desire of one's own heart for the offender, but does not go beyond what is right. If Jesus and Stephen both pray for, rather than pronounce, forgiveness in respect of their unrepentant persecutors, we should not ask victims of abuse to pronounce forgiveness on abusers who have not yet repented, but rather to pray for them. This is in line with the teaching of Jesus; *"Love your enemies and pray for those who persecute you, so that you may be sons of your Father who is in heaven"* (Matt. 5.44-45).

Matthew 18, which we have used to outline many of the dynamics of child abuse, ends with issues of forgiveness (18.21-35). However the issue of forgiveness is not addressed until the issue of accountability has been pressed to the point of whole church discipline (18.15-18). The aim is to gain or win one's brother (18.15), but nowhere are we told to skip directly to the issue of forgiveness. Indeed, to do so is to be cruel to a person who has already been victimised. The issue of forgiveness will arise and is vital for the healing of the victim, but it does not happen as a stand-alone issue, as if forgiveness is the only or first issue. Effective forgiveness, that releases the victim from the perpetrator, is one part of a number of elements that bring true freedom, but it always deals with the prior issue of accountability (who is to blame?), and the current attitude of the offender (is there repentance?). Forgiveness does not happen in a vacuum.

The second circumstance is where the offender appears to be repentant but, after a lapse of time, re-offends. He then sins, repents, sins, and repents, until a cycle of repeat offending and what seems to be transitory guilt is established. How are we to cope with this situation? Each act of repentance, especially at the start of the process, seems to offer the victim hope that the offending will stop, only for these hopes to be dashed when the offence is repeated. It is easy to understand the cynicism that a victim might develop in these circumstances. Words become very cheap in this context. This is a very difficult position for the victim of whatever offence is being repeated, and I am very reluctant to apply this teaching to someone who is still a child. The earlier sections refer to an adult and **a little one** who is stumbled (18.6) and who subsequently strays (18.14). The section on forgiveness is introduced by Peter's question about forgiving my **brother**. The term *"brother"* is one of equality, while the term *"little one"* is one that underlines inequality in status. The section on forgiveness is to do with relationships between adults, and should not be rigidly imposed on children and their relationship to key adults in their lives.

Having said that, the teaching of Jesus here is clear; when I am faced by repeated requests for forgiveness, I should forgive even if past experience tells me that there is unlikely to be permanent change of behaviour towards me. That we are dealing with requested forgiveness is even clearer in Luke 17.3-4; *"if your brother sins, rebuke him, and if he repents, forgive him; and if he sins against you seven times in the day,* ***and turns to you seven times, and says, 'I repent,'*** *you must forgive him".* The forgiveness is to be requested before forgiveness can be pronounced, but it is to be pronounced however many times it is requested. This does not mean that the victim is to trust the perpetrator again; it does not mean that forgiving is no big deal; it does not mean that everything will be as if the offence had never happened; it does not create amnesia; but it is giving up the right to right the wrong oneself, or to take revenge. I may have to involve others and, if the law has been broken, especially by an offence against a child, it may have to be dealt with by statutory bodies. It is, however, not a matter of personal revenge. Absalom has shown us the futility of that line of action.

There is nothing in this teaching that requires someone who has been abused to stay compliantly in the place where she is vulnerable to further abuse, and where experience has shown that the offender is well able to sin again. It is a high calling to forgive repeated offences; maybe it is only as we remember that this is how the Father deals with his children, that we can find the motivation and strength to love this way. It is also possible that the repeated necessity for an offender to come and ask for forgiveness again and again, if met with genuine love and forgiveness, will convict him, not only of his originating sin, but also his shallowness, weakness and gross insincerity. Again, I feel it is necessary to underline that this responsibility to forgive is between brothers, that is, equals. It cannot simplistically be imposed on children who are the victims of repeated offences at the hands of significant adults in their lives, and in comparison to whom they are relatively powerless.

The third circumstance is where the perpetrator comes to the place of genuine repentance. It might appear that this situation is relatively simple, but this too involves a major task for the victim. The best example is in the story of the Prodigal Son. The task for the father is to maintain a forgiving spirit towards his son for an indefinite period, while he cannot be sure whether or not his son will ever return. This waiting in 'hope-pain' is the attitude of true prayer for forgiveness. The embrace of the son and the welcome home can **only** come when the son returns in heart and on foot. The father does not know how long he will have to wait. That is why his faith is stretched in the process. The passion of the embrace is only possible because the father has won the battle of patient waiting in hope. The son's real and demonstrated repentance, in the end, frees the father to pronounce what was in his heart all along, *"this my son… was lost and is found"* (Lk.15.24). It is not just victims that are strays, so are perpetrators. The self-control of the father as he waits is part of his exuberance when he welcomes the son home. Forgiveness takes time and process to be effective and real. We cannot short-circuit the process and help the victim any more than forcing the butterfly out of its chrysalis helps it to fly. The journey to forgiveness will be travelled or avoided; but it cannot be truncated by magic or by well-meaning friends.

Just as forgiveness is a journey, so it is not, automatically, ground taken, never to be lost again. It is a commitment to live in forgiveness towards the offender. It is a commitment to continue in forgiveness, and to see forgiveness as a long-term issue, not just an act at a point in time. Is it not wonderful that this is the quality of the Lord's attitude towards us? We are left with two further considerations. What about the issue of forgiving God? And what about the issue of forgiving ourselves?

Forgiving God

I am extremely uneasy at any teaching that states or implies that there could be circumstances in which we should have to forgive God. To do so is to infer that God is at fault in some way. God is not by nature or character, by omission or commission 'at fault'. To say that we forgive Him is to imply that we project fault onto Him, which means that the whole exercise is based on a false premise. Such contortions cannot be healing in their nature, as they are not based in truth. Any appearance of healing or sense of healing that ensued would have to be interpreted in a different way. It dare not be the sense of having taken the moral high ground by forgiving, for we can never be in such a position in relation to God.

There are no Biblical instances of a man or woman forgiving God. There are expressions of confusion and hurt towards God as the writer struggles to come to terms with hard events in his life. *"O God, why dost thou cast us off for ever?"* (Ps. 74.1), *"How long, O Lord, wilt thou look on? Rescue me from their ravages, my life from the lions!"* (Ps. 35.17), and the heart cry of the prophet and the Son, *"My God, My God, why hast thou forsaken me?"* (Ps. 22.1; Matt. 27.46). They feel that God has abandoned, ignored or forsaken them, but this cry never leads to the conclusion that God is, in fact, guilty of doing so, thus he does not need to be forgiven. Indeed, if we say we forgive God, we infer that God, to do the thing right, should have asked for our forgiveness! And, if what was said above is correct, we should wait until he does ask before we can effectively pronounce forgiveness on Him! This way of thinking seems to me to verge on blasphemy, and is at the very least highly dangerous.

In Psalm 74 Asaph reminds God of his covenant (v20), of the need of the innocent, (v21), of the insult that the oppressor is directing towards God himself (not just at the victims), and he continues to pray, though, at the end of the Psalm, the answer has not yet come. There is no mention of blaming or forgiving God, only of the struggle to understand God's ways. In Psalm 35 David states his confidence that God has seen the injustice (v22), prays for his own vindication (v24) and the downfall of his enemies (v26), but he envisages the day when his tongue shall tell of God's righteousness, and praise him all the day long. Again there is no mention of blame or the need to forgive God. Psalm 22 actually describes, prophetically, the judgement of God against our sin as it falls on the Son of God. From Jesus' perspective the punishment is unjust because he never sinned; he did not deserve it. Yet even he proclaims that God *"has not despised or abhorred the affliction of the afflicted; and he has not hid his face from him, but has heard, when he cried to him".* (v24). There is nothing for which he has to forgive God in all he went through. Interestingly, God heard when he cried, though we know that the deliverance was a resurrection that took place later. What would have happened if Jesus had pointed the finger at God and accused him of being a perpetrator?

Forgiving Self

The issue of forgiving oneself is also important. It is a fact that many victims of child sexual abuse feel partly or fully to blame for the abuse they experienced. The way of acting and speaking adopted by the perpetrator infuses these notions in the most insidious ways, but we have already seen that Jesus does not impute blame to the little ones who are stumbled (Matt 18). Such guilt is psychological only. That does not mean that it is not felt as real by the victim; it is, but the feelings of the victim do not infallibly define the truth of the situation, and the remedy here is to do with reallocation of responsibility to the perpetrator and effective forgiveness of him, rather than self condemnation and the struggle to forgive self. If, in reaction to abuse, a victim sins in attitude or deed, repentance may well be needed for that, but it is never for the abuse itself.

Child Sexual Abuse and the Gospel

Self-condemnation often expresses false guilt taken on board from the offender or sometimes, possibly, an inadequate grasp of the complete all-encompassing grace of God that cleanses the sinner who turns to him in relation to matters that are his true responsibility. Regret and self-recrimination for having unintentionally put oneself at risk are not the same as guilt. Tamar could have regretted her naivety and beaten herself up over her decision to help Amnon, and her failure to see the situation that was developing. But there was no disobedience on her part and so there was no guilt. Better than self-punishment for lack of foresight, is the decision to learn from the experience, no matter how painful. To feel a need to forgive oneself is to accept guilt and responsibility that in God's books are invoiced to the account of the perpetrator. Although it should not be called self-forgiveness, there is a need to let go the desire to blame self and to criticise what may only have been naivety and good faith. None of us can relive the past; but we can repeat it if we do not learn from it, and we can find ourselves stuck in it, if we do not work our way through these issues. Both are ways that, in effect, resist the healing-growing process.

The issue of forgiveness is complex, and we have considered a number of the more subtle struggles that can be present for a victim of abuse. Let us not make the imperative to forgive a shallow or quick remedy; it is not, and it sometimes needs time, patience and support to walk that journey to a healthy outcome. More than we ever imagined can be learnt about the heart of God in the forgiveness process, **if** we can remain open to him as we journey.

Shame

There is often the related issue of shame. I will define shame as a sense of distress or humiliation caused by consciousness of the guilt of an associate. It involves taking on the negative consequences of the wrong done by those close to us, and even the wrong done to us by others. It is the sense of being personally spoiled by the wrongdoing of another. As I understand it, shame does not imply personal guilt. Jesus endured the shame of the cross because he was identified with us, and with our sin (Heb 12.2). It was surely not for anything that he had done. Shame for the child abuse victim means experiencing the fallout of the actions of another. There is also the element of it becoming public or, we could say, a sense of nakedness (Is 47.3). That is why, from the beginning, there has been a profound tendency to hide as a response to shame (Gen 3.7). Shame is not the same as guilt, though they can be mixed in experience in ways difficult to disentangle. There are even differences between shame-based and guilt-based cultures, ours being the latter, which may make shame more difficult for us to understand and deal with.

In marriage unashamed nakedness was part of the created order (Gen 2.25). We believe that it is also part of the redemptive order, and the birthright of every believer. The other possibility is to become shameless or brazen, but that is the pathway to falling. *"Were they ashamed when they committed abominations? No, they were not at all ashamed; they did not know how to blush. Therefore they shall fall among those who fall"* (Jer. 6.15). There are even those who *"glory in their shame"* (Phil 3.19) to their own destruction. Such a response is to deny the power of the cross to transform ones life (Phil 3.18), for the cross is the answer to shame as much as for guilt. The cross restores us to relationship with the only one whose opinion of us matters, the Father, and he sees us as family. *"Fear not, for you will not be ashamed; be not confounded, for you will not be put to shame; for you will forget the shame of your youth, and the reproach of your widowhood you will remember no more. For your Maker is your husband, the Lord of Hosts is his name; and the Holy One of Israel is your Redeemer, the God of the whole earth he is called"* (Is 54.4-5).

It is often the legitimate needs of the victim that are contaminated by the shame of association with the perpetrator. For example, the child who is abused is one who is already vulnerable. The valid needs of this child to be special, to be loved, and to belong may be exploited and manipulated by the offender to his own ends and for his own gratification. In the process what was a legitimate need is tarnished by the exploitation. We are created as sexual beings but abuse as a child may spoil the experience of sex as an adult by making it a thing of fear and aversion, or an area without boundaries or safety. Shame can both spoil and rob what was to be good in its right place. This can deeply affect the quality of intimacy in marriage, as we shall see.

The Leaving, Cleaving, One-Flesh Process

The need for pastoral help often does not arise in a one-to-one context, but in the situation of marriage difficulties that stem from one partner's experience of child sexual abuse. Here the dysfunction in the current relationship pushes the parties to face the unresolved issues in important past relationships. There are a number of ways this unconscious connection between past and present can occur. Normal sexual activity in the marriage can recapitulate forms of approach or touch that trigger past experiences into the present and cause one party to freeze or to push away the other. As this is often an automatic response, and if the couple have not shared what happened in the past, both can be puzzled, hurt and offended by the close down of normal marital expectations. What was meant to be pleasurable becomes fraught, and can undermine the relationship. At this point some people start to face past abuse and begin to seek help. The issue therefore needs to be reframed in the context of the marriage, rather than being seen as purely an individual matter.

The Biblical process of marriage formation is to leave, to cleave and to become one flesh (Gen 2.24). This principle is so fundamental to establishing a healthy marriage that it is referred to three times in the New Testament in response to different issues. Paul quotes this verse in Ephesians to establish it as the basis for forming a marriage, and draws the well-known parallel to the relationship between Christ and the church (Eph. 5.30-31). He also uses it as the basis of his teaching against casual sex (1 Cor. 6.16), and Jesus uses the same starting point to address the issue of divorce and remarriage (Matt 19.5-6).

Especially if the sexual abuse of childhood is at the hands of a father or father figure, there can be the tendency for a girl to generalise her resultant attitude to all males, creating reservation and distrust towards those who come into key roles in her life, such as her husband. Her expectation and perception of her husband are formed or influenced by her experience of her father (or abuser), and his presence is unconsciously carried through into the marriage. Sometimes this leads to her selecting a partner who fulfils that expectation and who will re-enact the same model of maleness as she has known. Sometimes she may project attributes onto her husband that are not really there, and react to them as if they were. The husband in this case is at a loss to understand what is happening between them. The truth is that we all do this to some extent, because we each have to leave our father and mother, with all the expectations they have socialised into us, and cleave to the partner who is actually there, which means not projecting but really seeing our partner. If we cannot negotiate this process our mental picture of our partner will jar with who our partner really is, and there will be dissonance. Dissonance never enhances the sexual relationship; it creates the circumstance in which we can use the physical intimacy and vulnerability of the sexual union to hurt the other, whether deliberately or inadvertently. In other words, sexual problems often flag up that there are leaving and cleaving problems.

Ezekiel 16 gives us the picture of a girl abandoned at birth, totally rejected and uncared for (Ezek. 16.1-5). This passage is in the form of an allegory or parable. It is a typical human story illustrating spiritual realities from God's perspective. He is communicating with us on the basis of what we already know from life to give a message about the bigger dimension that the story is being used to convey. The same is true for example in the parable of the Prodigal Son. However, it only works as an effective vehicle for spiritual truth because it is also true to life. It therefore can be seen as speaking to us equally on two levels. From this perspective Ezekiel 16 gives insight into the inner dynamics of a deeply rejected woman and her tempestuous journey to forgiveness and healing, as well as being a prophetic vehicle for speaking to a people unfaithful to their God.

Abused emotionally, abandoned and rejected, she eventually grows to physical maturity and marries. But her physical maturity and beauty are not matched by emotional maturity. She makes for herself *"images of men"*(RSV)(16.17) with which she gets sexually involved. Literal idolatry for Jerusalem but, for such a rejected woman at the human level, this is more a mental form of idolatry, a variety of fantasy creation in her mind which projects idealised qualities onto whatever partner she engages with. In Western society we do not carve images, we form relatively unconscious mental constructs that have the same function. In real life this process is not uncommon and leads to the young woman entering serial relationships with unsuitable men, none of whom turn out to be what she dreams they are. The real man in front of her is not well motivated, being only out to satisfy his own needs, but she sees an idealised picture of him in her mind, that is until reality shatters it and she looks for the next 'knight in shining armour' to appear over the hill.

We are told that the compulsive reason she pursued this self-destructive path, in a series of bad relationships, is that she was *"insatiable", "still not satisfied,"* and *"lovesick"* (16.28-30)(RSV). She had a compelling inner need that drove her to grab at happiness, and prevented her from making any realistic evaluation of the type of man she was reaching for. The fact that the woman might be married to a good husband (in the parable Jehovah is the husband of Jerusalem) is not the point. She is so damaged that she cannot, yet, receive or even see him as he is. She has not left her parents so she cannot cleave to her husband, and so goes after illusionary relationships not knowing that what she really needs is there.

Absorption with her fantasy about her male friends places her children below her horizon of concern, and they are as a result sacrificed to these need-based relationships. *"And you took your sons and your daughters, whom you had borne to me, and these you sacrificed to them to be devoured"* (16.20). Few such males, that is those who are preying on vulnerable women, have much interest in the offspring of her previous partners, and she has lost sight of her children's needs in the pink haze of the latest fantasy man in her life. When deep emotional needs are not met in infancy and childhood they clamour all the more for attention in later life. These unmet needs block awareness of the equally real needs of her own dependant children who are emotionally deprived in turn. In family and child care work I saw this pattern repeated many times.

This woman, however, has done two key things that have been her decisive steps in getting into this position; it has not just happened to her. Firstly she *"trusted in (her) beauty"* (16.15). She was physically beautiful, but that was the only part of her person in which she had any confidence. Her inner emotional resources were so impaired by her early experience of people and life that she had nothing else to build on. The second decisive element was that she *"did not remember the days of her youth"* (16.22,43). Her childhood was too painful to face and resolve, so she suppressed the experience, only for it to drive her current behaviour from beneath the surface. She was not being promiscuous for gain (16.34), but out of deep unmet emotional needs, and she could not see that any number of sexual liaisons could never touch that need. Because she could not face and learn from her past, especially facing her experience with her parents, she cannot leave them or cleave to her husband. In fact she becomes like her mother who loathed her husband and her children (16.45-46). There is much more in this example that time and focus require us to pass over at this point, but she is forgiven and restored by the end of the passage

Child Sexual Abuse and the Gospel

(16.63). Once we are in a marriage these issues of leaving and cleaving are the fabric of the relationships we have to work out. The more we do so successfully, the more we are free to cleave and experience one-flesh fulfilment with our partner.

It should be obvious that child sexual abuse, which always includes elements of emotional abuse in some way, will be likely to intrude into the marriage relationship at its most sensitive point. It is the responsibility of the one who was the victim of abuse to deal with this issue; no one else can do the work for her. An example will illustrate this. Janice came to a seminar we were taking on the subject of child sexual abuse. She later contacted us to seek help. She was the youngest of several daughters and had been sexually abused by her father following the premature death of her mother. She had, as an adult, told her sisters of her abuse and discovered that none of her older siblings reported similar abuse, probably because they were old enough to have left home or to deal with the pressure by that time. In spite of this Janice had been left to make the arrangements for her father's funeral because she lived closest to him. When she came to see us about six weeks after the funeral, she was struggling with why her sisters had done this to her in spite of knowing about her abuse. The past abuse and her internal turmoil regarding the funeral were adversely affecting her marriage.

When she arrived, Janice recounted a vivid dream that she had experienced several nights before. In the dream she and her husband were on either side of her father's deathbed. Janice was standing and speaking to her father. She was telling him that he was wrong to have abused her, that she had been hurt by his offending, and that it was his fault, not hers, that the abuse had taken place. This 'telling' was repeated a number of times. She told us that she had never been able to do this in real life, and could not understand why she should have such a dream after he had died. We asked her whether there had been any change in her relationship with her husband since the dream, and, again quite surprised and a little embarrassed, she told us that the intimate side of her marriage had greatly improved.

We pointed out what seemed to be the obvious explanation of the process she was in. Firstly, she had, for the first time, given herself permission to reallocate responsibility for the abuse onto her father where it belonged. She had never dared to do this while he was still alive. His death had created enough of a sense of safety for her to be able to 'confront' him, and blame him for the first time. As we saw above, it is necessary to reallocate responsibility in order both to forgive, on the one hand, and to disentangle areas of our own responsibility, on the other, usually relating to negative or resentful attitudes. For her it took a God-given dream to unlock the process. The fact that she was standing over him and the repeated way in which she spoke to her father in the dream underlined the clarity with which she was doing the necessary work. This also emphasises that there can be substantial healing even though the offender has died and no reconciliation, at least in this life, is possible.

Secondly, the scene showed the position of her father in her marriage. He was between her and her husband. He was nearer to her than her husband. He was in the bed, not the couple. While the bed was his deathbed, it also seemed to symbolise the intimacy of their marriage, and the fact that they could not find this together. To see her husband, she had to look past her father. The father was intruding between husband and wife. Thirdly, all that she was saying in the dream was being said in front of her husband. He could hear what she was saying, and this openness of communication has to be at the heart of any progress in the level of understanding between them in their marriage. In the dream she was quite unashamed in speaking as she did, and it felt liberating to her. Afterwards it was easier to talk to the real person to whom she was married. This is cleaving, made possible by the elements of leaving she was enacting towards her father. No wonder the sexual relationship improved spontaneously.

The final observation was that the combination of circumstances showed that God was working to bless and free her. The seminar, her father's death, the dream, and the discussion came together to bring deep issues to light and help her take great steps forward. The most telling fact about the dream was that she was the only active participant. Both her father and her husband were hearing but were not active in doing anything. This is as it should be; the responsibility for leaving (facing, reallocating responsibility and accurately forgiving) was hers, as it is for each person who becomes an adult. No one else can do this work for us; we each have to do it for ourselves. Someone may push me overboard into the sea, and it is clear that it is not my fault that I am drowning. But, when the lifebelt is thrown in to me, it is my responsibility, and mine alone, to grasp it and to take responsibility for doing all I can to co-operate with being rescued. The child was not responsible for being abused but, as an adult, needs to take responsibility for seeking to be healed. The experience of healing is a major contribution to improvement in the marriage.

Saving your Life, or Losing your Life?

The Gospel is that there is a Saviour so, not only am I unable to save myself, I do not even have to try. In fact, the things I do to try to save myself all, ultimately, hinder the One who wants to save me. In the area of child sexual abuse, victims and perpetrators devise many strategies to 'save themselves.' These are understandable but counterproductive in the end. When I was a social work team leader, one little girl was admitted to care because of severe neglect that did not show improvement, even after substantial input of resources. She was admitted with only one item she herself owned, a dirty rag dolly. Her new foster mum took her to buy clothes and basic necessities, and also wanted to buy the little girl a new doll, thinking that she would be delighted. The little girl became very upset at the thought of giving away her old dolly, so her foster mother wisely dropped the issue and went home. She informed the social worker of what had happened and it was agreed not to make an issue of the doll.

Child Sexual Abuse and the Gospel

Over the next year the little girl gradually grew in confidence in her new home, and began to disclose things she remembered about her family, culminating in the disclosure of sexual abuse by her mother's partner. She described this as happening after she went to bed at night when he came in to kiss her goodnight. The foster mother and the social worker were aware by this time that she always took her dolly to bed with her, and could not go otherwise. It became clear, as a result of further work with the little girl, that the dolly was her escape route during the abuse. She would cuddle and protect the dolly in her arms, to the point that it seemed as if she were hiding her inner self in the dolly and trying to protect herself. The importance of the dolly to her became very clear, and we were so pleased not to have forced the issue shortly after placement. The little girl was given a safe place to talk about her experience and find that she was now indeed safe in her new family. I remember the day when the social worker came to tell me that this little girl had gone to her foster mum and had handed her the old dolly. She had then asked if it would be all right to get a new one now. All we could do was to sit and cry together. I have never experienced a more poignant illustration of the new-for-old message that is the Gospel, but we have to let the old go to the Saviour, and to stop trying to save ourselves, to experience the new. We can try to hold on to the old life, under the guise of protecting ourselves, to the point where we cannot move on.

There are many ways that a victim can try to 'save herself'. One is pleasure seeking; that is trying to replace the inner pain with pleasure, and having to grab more and more to squash the pain out of her consciousness. Alcohol and drug addictions can come about from the same motivation to self-anaesthesia. The repression of painful memories, like the girl in Ezekiel 16, is an attempt to save herself from the worst of her inner pain, but again it serves only to multiply the sources of pain in her life. Unforgiveness and revenge give a focus and outlet for pain, but these tend to be destructive and precipitate more misery. Self-pity can lead to many forms of compensatory behaviour towards self, and to a generalised lack of trust in others in a way that does not discriminate. If the victim can keep people out, maybe she can avoid being hurt again. Unfortunately this involves keeping life out as well, because good relationships make a good life.

All of these strategies, and more, are unconscious for the most part, and all make a certain sense when we understand the hurt that the victim has experienced, but all of them get in the way of true healing and change. Lot's wife could or would not let the past go, and lost her life. *"Remember Lot's wife. Whoever seeks to gain his life will lose it, but whoever loses his life will preserve it"* (Lk. 17.32-33). In the context of the closest of family relationships, Jesus says that we have to love him more, and put him first, and this letting go is summarised as follows: - *"He who finds his life will lose it, and he who loses his life for my sake will find it"* (Matt 10.39). The Lord wants to come between the victim and key family members or significant others, whether her attitude to them is negative or positive.

Child Sexual Abuse and the Gospel

Finally, if we let our life go as a seed, it falls into the ground and dies; but it bears much fruit. Some of us want our old life to die, but we are afraid that there is no new life to replace it. The claim of the Gospel is that only by this way is there new life, and the added bonus of fruitfulness. The greatest pain can be turned to fruitful living if we let the old go into the hands of the One who can save us. When we bear fruit from the soil of pain and difficulty we are no longer victims, or even survivors, but over-comers, just as he overcame. Are we willing for the Gospel to work its full effect in us? It may be costly but it is priceless.

We have, from an individual and pastoral perspective, considered some of the issues that can be encountered in overcoming the impact of sexual abuse and its repercussions in the adult life of one who was a victim of child sexual abuse. We can even re-weave the experiences of abuse into life in a way that deepens our experience of much that is good, and creates in us a resource for others - a bringing of treasure out of darkness. There is, however, also a corporate and governmental perspective when this issue is uncovered within the sphere of the local congregation. The next and final section turns to these concerns.

Notes. 1. Lewis, C.S., "The Great Divorce", Collins, 1946. P 61-63 - The conversation with George McDonald.

SECTION THREE

CHILD SEXUAL ABUSE

AND THE

LOCAL CHURCH

Chapter Nine

Fit for Purpose and Ready to Respond

It tends to be the case that congregations that are thriving and vibrant attract many young people and families, and, as a consequence, have a popular youth and children's work in place. It is also the case that people with a sexual orientation towards children are attracted to situations where there is easy access to children. It therefore follows that thriving congregations, with many children and young people, are the most vulnerable congregations. It may also be that congregations, where there is a sense of life and the testimony of lives being changed, attract people with serious problems who hope that somehow God might intervene and change them. Whether for good reasons or evil, or a mixture of both, those with paedophile inclinations are likely to gravitate to places where there is the blessing of young life.

The advent of Sex Offender legislation in 1997 in the UK, led to the post-sentence monitoring and risk management of child sex offenders by groups of professionals from the Police, Social Services, the Probation Service, and the Housing Authority. Hitherto untracked groups of individuals were, as a result, monitored in an on-going way for the first time. In the area in which I worked I became very concerned at how many surfaced, at least for part of their life, in a local church congregation. This was the main reason that I resigned from my career in Social Services to set up Family Spectrum, the purpose of which is to help the local church address and manage such complex family threatening problems as these. If our congregations are so attractive and vulnerable to those who would pose a risk to the young, we have a duty before God to be fit for purpose and ready to respond.

Any congregation that is properly positioned to handle the full range of child protection and child abuse issues will have to have a number of things in place. The most obvious is an adequate Child Protection Policy and Procedure. This is now generally accepted, and will include provisions for the children's work and young people's work in the church. Youth leaders need to know what to be concerned about, and what to do should concern arise about the well-being of a child, or the behaviour of another leader. Lines of accountability should be clear and there should be someone in the church who fills the role of child protection co-ordinator, to whom youth leaders are accountable, and who will liase with the leadership of the church and, if necessary, the statutory authorities should an issue occur.

However if the existence of Child Protection Procedures is the only provision, it makes the congregation more vulnerable not less. The reason for this is that the congregation may relax as if it were now safer, when it is, in fact, just more accountable. It is the depth of understanding and awareness in the people, especially the leadership team, and the willingness to address tough issues, that provides the best protection and most effective responses should something happen. Procedures are a useful guide to people who are properly motivated in the first place. Youth leader training should accompany the policy and procedures, to alert the leaders to the subtlety of this issue, and to the signals or concerns that should trigger a response. The skills to respond to a child who wants to confide, or who behaves in a way that causes concern, start at the point when the very first word is said. Immediate responses will tend either to encourage the child to talk or to close the child down. At this point the biggest issue is the internal poise and positioning of the leader towards the child, which helps the child have the confidence to speak, or otherwise. This poise, generally, is not achieved well without training and thought before hand.

A congregation also needs adequate pastoral resources to help those who are now adults but who were abused as children. These needs may not be immediately apparent but can be flushed to the surface by personal life events, or by issues emerging in the congregation. The training of home group leaders and a pastoral team is important. Most parents want to be able to 'street-proof' their children against approaches that are dangerous, equipping them with the knowledge of how to react in such circumstances. Yet they often need help to be able to talk to their children in a language and in a way that does not repel them or make them fearful. Parents want this help and a congregation is an ideal place to work with groups of parents to this end.

The single most important factor in achieving maximum safety in a congregation is the degree of ownership of responsibility taken by the leadership team. I have met many congregational child protection co-ordinators who feel isolated from support from the minister/pastor/eldership or leadership team. They feel that they have been appointed to take the heat off the leaders, whose focus is on many other important things. Unsupported co-ordinators tend to burn out quickly and resign from the role as a result. This leads to a loss of skill, and the introduction of new people into the role, only for them to experience the same lack of support in their turn.

Apart from general responsibility to ensure that child protection and pastoral care are covered in the church, the leaders are likely to be involved in any child protection investigation into a family in the congregation, in any allegation against a youth leader, and in any situation where an offender surfaces in the congregation. How they handle these issues can determine the credibility of their future ministry. I remember the situation of a child in care who attended a church based uniformed organisation. His foster carers were members of the church. During the interval at the annual display of the youth organisation, the inspecting officer sexually abused the lad in the toilets. Fortunately, the young man told his carers, who reported the incident, leading to a full investigation.

Child Sexual Abuse and the Local Church

The man acting as inspecting officer was from a different congregation. The minister of his home congregation was approached as part of the investigation, and he informed social work staff that a similar incident had occurred while the man was an officer in the youth organisation in his home church. When this had come to light some time previously, the minister 'had spoken to him' and had 'dealt with the issue.' This was probably to avoid the adverse publicity that would have focussed on his church. As it was, the irresponsibility of the minister led to an offender being left free to continue to operate in the context of youth work. In addition, the initial victim was left feeling sidelined and devalued by the minister's approach, and a further young man was victimised in another congregation. The resulting scandal was bigger than it might otherwise have been, and the publicity did more damage to the reputation of the minister and congregation than it need have. What he feared came on him, because he did not have the understanding or the backbone to deal with the issue first time round. He lost his credibility while trying to save it; does this sound familiar? I recognise that most leaders, even those who have had several years of formal theological training, have **not** been trained in these issues. That is no excuse. There are now many options available to access this input and it is the duty of the leadership team to ensure that all necessary elements are in place in, or available to, the congregation. Please remember what Jesus said about not despising these little ones; it can be done by neglect as much as by commission.

We should not be surprised if leaders find it difficult to take on board the importance of child protection; the twelve disciples were exactly the same. After all the teaching that Jesus had given them in Matthew 18 about the importance of not stumbling the little ones, and the revelation that our attitude to children is our attitude to Christ (18.6), one would have thought that the disciples would have got the message. They did not. In the **next** chapter it says: - *"Then children were brought to him that he might lay his hands on them and pray. The disciples rebuked the people; but Jesus said, 'Let the children come to me, and do not hinder them; for to such belongs the kingdom of heaven,' And he laid his hands on them and went away"* (Matt.19.13-15). In Jesus' opinion the disciples were still hindering the children. One of the things that have grieved me most is the number of people we have met who were first abused just before or shortly after their first response in faith to Christ. This is surely the enemy's work. To hinder the children is not to abuse them, but it comes out of a low value placed on children, and the deceptive idea that the Lord of Glory is more preoccupied with 'more important matters.' He is not, and neither should we be.

There are several major issues that can make it more difficult for a Christian leader to act responsibly in this area. These are the issues of authority, of theology, of church discipline, and of inter-church and inter-ministry co-operation, and we need to consider how these interplay.

Child Sexual Abuse and the Local Church
Authority

There are several strands to this issue. The first is the relationship between the spiritual authority vested in the church and the civil authority vested in the powers that be. All Christian traditions see both realms of authority as delegated from God.[1] We live in a context where there is a highly developed, perhaps overdeveloped, body of legislation with subsidiary regulations, and then policies and procedures to direct the way in which public officials and citizens address certain problems. This is certainly true in the area of child protection. We are a democratic society, but not all cultures or societies are, and the New Testament was not written in that context. We believe that the powers that be are instituted by God (Rom 13.1), and ultimately accountable to him. However, they do not always appear to legislate in harmony with the will of God as revealed in his word. What then is our attitude towards them to be? Do we argue that we must obey God rather than man and take the consequences? Do we comply without protest or consideration of the Biblical position? Or do we take each issue on its merits and seek to be good citizens without breaching conscience in the process? Our understanding of the relationship between state and church, and what is the nature of church, colours these issues. Then our denominational structure of authority, or our non-denominational independence, also determine where authority, and therefore responsibility, lies. I do not want here to argue one form of church government against another, only to note that authority and responsibility are tied together, and that that will create different strains in different denominational contexts.

My starting point is that the authority vested by God in the state is valid authority, and so we have a duty of respect towards the officers of the state in all circumstances, and of obedience in all situations except where this would contravene the Word of God. This is, however, only the starting point, because few Biblical Christians would take issue so far. As a young social worker, I really struggled for a time with this issue. It was crystallized for me by Dr Jay Adams, who was a minister in three Presbyterian denominations in the US, later becoming Associate Professor of Practical Theology at Westminster Theological Seminary, and a well-known exponent of Christian Counselling. I had the opportunity to meet him twice in Northern Ireland and to discuss at length his position, which he would have described as 'Reformed'. In this view God instituted the state to be a terror to bad conduct (Rom 13.3), and to execute the wrath of God on the wrongdoer (13.4). This, in his view, limited the function of the state to the law and order agenda. The provision of support services, counselling and education, for example, were not seen as responsibilities that God had delegated to the state, but to the church. For him it followed that anyone with a sense of call in these areas should exercise that call in the context of the church, not in state sponsored activities. This would have ruled me out as a statutory social worker, and Dr Adams confirmed that, in his view, this was so. Clearly, in his view, the state had over stretched its arm into many areas of human activity beyond the sphere authorised them by God. This seemed to make suspect at best the position of those agencies that do provide services and counsel on a statutory basis. One would suspect that churches, theologically suspicious of an agency of the state, are less likely to welcome the input of the agency, and less likely to provide co-operation with its activities. In this theological view it is, however, acceptable for Christians to serve in the police, armed services and judiciary, as these are the functions legitimately delegated by God to the state for the maintenance of law and order.

Shortly after this I had opportunity to stay in the Mennonite Centre in London and be in dialogue with the staff there. A whole new theological approach opened up that went in the reverse direction. Their argument was based on the presumption that our obligations as citizens of the kingdom of heaven superseded any duties required of us by a lower authority, including that of the state. This would preclude a Christian taking on any responsibilities for the civil authorities that were contradicted by what is required of citizens of God's kingdom. Specifically, the injunction to turn the other cheek, which is expected kingdom behaviour (Matt 5.39), could not be compatible with the duties of those who serve in the police or armed services of any state, where the implication is that there must be a readiness to use force when required. However, those arms of the state that provided services, help and counsel, and that did not require the direct exercise of force or violence, were compatible, or more compatible, with the ethos of the Gospel and the kingdom. Police and army service are ruled out and social work is ruled in! Clearly the arguments on both sides are more intricate than typified here, and I am not arguing for one or other position, though the fact I worked in social services for over thirty years implies how I resolved the issues for myself; but I am trying to show that theological position colours how we see the agencies of the state, those who work in them and our inclination to work with them, and that this has great impact in the field of child protection.

I have since found a third theological perspective that also affects perceptions in this area. Within the Charismatic community (and others) there is the tendency, not incorrectly, to take the scriptures as speaking to individuals directly. The Christian community identifies with the promises to Israel and even sees itself as the current expression of God's holy nation, 'Israel', or 'Zion'. Alongside this flows the perception that the secular context in which we live is 'Egypt', the kingdom of Pharaoh, or 'Babylon'. We know that Pharaoh sought counsel and enlightenment from a collection of wizards and soothsayers deeply involved in the occult and black magic. We tie that in with the New Testament view that principalities and powers are fallen angelic hierarchies that pull the strings of human affairs from unseen realms *"in the heavenlies"*, primarily expressed through the governmental structures in a nation. We thereby set in opposition the people of God, the church, on the one hand, and the fallen world government in society on the other, in a polarised spiritual battle, where we are either for or against.

Child Sexual Abuse and the Local Church

There is truth in this perception, but it can lead us to places the New Testament does not go. Paul would have reason to distrust and fear the emperor and his delegates (they eventually killed him), and it was he who described the fallen angelic principalities and powers as demonic (Eph 6.11-20), yet he enjoins a very different attitude towards those exercising authority in the state. He says, *"we are not contending against flesh and blood, but against the principalities, against the powers, against the world rulers of this present darkness, against the spiritual hosts of wickedness in the heavenly places"* (Eph. 6.12). But he also says, *"Remind them to be submissive to rulers and authorities, to be obedient, to be ready for any honest work, to speak evil of no one, to avoid quarrelling, to be gentle, and to show perfect courtesy toward all men"* (Tit 3.1-2). He urges Timothy first of all to pray **for, not against**, kings and all who are in high positions (1 Tim 2.1-2), as clearly as he urges us to resist the demonic authorities in the heavenlies. There is to be a very different attitude towards the spiritual principalities and the institution of the state operated by men. The former we are to resist, and the latter we are to submit to and co-operate with as best we can from our side. This is true, whether the agencies of the state are sympathetic to us or not. If we perceive state agencies as agents of demonic forces we will not be motivated to work with them. If we see them as servants of God for the common good (Rom 13.4) we will have the attitude of allowing each his own legitimate area of authority, respecting that, and working with it.

But some have said to me that there are many occasions when the agents of the state have abused or abdicated their authority, so how can they be respected or submitted to. This initial statement is true; sometimes, in the area of child protection, the authorities have acted too quickly without an adequate legal basis, or too slowly to the hurt of children left unprotected. But so has the church, and with less excuse, because of the presence of Christ we claim we have. What do we say when Christian leaders have abused children? I have dealt with nearly thirty such cases. What do we say when those in Christian work, who have offended against children, are moved rather than reproved? I was involved in the investigation of a situation where a Christian worker in a children's ministry sexually abused a child in a swimming pool. He admitted the offence and was convicted. His organisation allowed him to continue in the same type of work, but moved him to another country with less well-developed child protection arrangements. Human error and frailty are a feature of church life as much as in state agencies. My experience is that those who work in state agencies are, in general, more willing than the church to openly acknowledge shortcomings and deal with them transparently. On the positive side, I have also had experience of Christian fellowships getting alongside and involved where children have been abused, and they have contributed much by being part of the protection plan, rather than part of the problem. It is not difficult to work out which approach is a better testimony to the family involved and to the professionals working to protect the children.

There is a further issue of authority and responsibility to consider. Some denominations have a hierarchical authority system where an external figure, such as a bishop, can make decisions about the internal workings of a congregation. At the other end of the spectrum there are independent fellowships led by a group of elders, or even more risky, by a single pastor accountable to no one. Some have a balance of internal and external (apostolic?) authority. Then there are individual differences between leaders because of how each man exercises his ministry, even within the same structure, and from the same theological background. Child sex offenders are not in church for reasons of theology or church government, and it causes them no great concern to move from one setting to another, in any theological or organisational direction. For leaders in whatever structure the issue of child abuse is fraught, but **responsibility rests at the place of authority,** whether this is within or outside the local congregation. There also is a sense in which all of us have responsibility to flag up concerns, but the leaders have the duty to make decisions and to act in child protective ways. Whoever becomes aware of an incident of abuse, has a responsibility to bring that to the attention of those in charge. But it is the leaders who have the responsibility to decide what is to be done to protect, to counsel, to discipline and to restore, and to represent the congregation to statutory agencies and the media if the matter becomes public.

Confidentiality and Discipline

Confidentiality is a strong value within the church and in professional practice alike. *"He who forgives an offence seeks love, but he who repeats a matter alienates a friend"* (Prov. 17.9), and *"Love covers a multitude of sins"* (1 Pet 4.8). The legal position in our society is that the only place of absolute confidentiality is in the lawyer-client relationship. Not even the church confessional is legally exempt.

Then there is the consideration that not all sin is illegal. For example adultery is sin but it is not a crime; it is civil wrong rather than a criminal matter in our culture. There is also a distinction between a man who voluntarily confesses a sin (James 5.16), and a man who is caught out in a sin, which he may well have continued in had he not been caught. The former shows a desire to genuinely repent from the outset, the latter may only be trying to limit damage by appearing contrite because he has been exposed. Evaluating the quality of remorse, contrition and repentance is therefore required. Again it may be clearer what I should do when I am the one sinned against, but what do I do when I learn of a serious sin against another, especially if the other is a child or vulnerable person? How do we manage the dilemmas of confidentiality from a Biblical perspective?

We have, in Chapter Six above, looked at the case of the sex offender in the church at Corinth, whose victim was an adult. This was not a case of two adults or equals in consensual sin, but of a perpetrator and a victim as 2 Cor 7.12 makes plain. Paul became aware of the existence of this relationship in the church because it was reported to him by members of the church (1 Cor 5.1). It was not the only problem that he had been advised of second hand. Chloe's people had reported that there was significant infighting and quarrelling (1 Cor 1.11) and Paul addresses this at length in chapters one to four. The same people, at the instigation of Chloe, or perhaps a different group, alerted him to the other serious moral problem that was distressing some in the church. What is remarkable is that Paul accepts the report as accurate without double-checking or independent corroboration. It is clear that there were several people in the group that reported these things to him, but it is equally clear that he writes a letter, inspired by the Holy Spirit, to address both issues **on the basis of this second hand information.** He does not reprove those who gave him the information for breaking confidence. It is also likely that the report, regarding the case of immorality, was itself based on second hand information, probably from the woman involved, rather than direct observation of any sinful act. Presumably they lived in the same home, but it is unlikely that someone actually saw them sleeping together.

Paul was the apostle who had planted the church, and his authority was recognised there, although not without competition between factions in the church (1.12), and from those who wished to be on a par with him in their ministries (2 Cor 11.4-5,13). He had a right to know and a duty to address the situation and, painful as it was both for him and the church, he does it (2 Cor 2.4-5). This involves him in making public his sources of information. The whole church will hear the reading of the letter and, if they did not know already, will hear who took the story to Paul. We do not know whether Chloe and her people were alerted beforehand that this would happen, or whether they were at ease with being identified as the 'lid lifters'. They may well have felt confirmed in the correctness of their actions because of Paul's response and his intended action, but this is reading between the lines. In any case they could not be assured of confidentiality any more than the family at the heart of this problem.

It is difficult to make public the internal dynamics of another family. The man concerned was living with his father's wife. Normally this would mean that the woman was his mother, but if that were so why not use the word 'mother'? It appears that the woman was his stepmother. This infers that his natural mother had been divorced or had died; I consider the latter more likely because of the Greek cultural customs around the value of the wife. Breiner records the following:- *"Demosthenes said, 'we have courtesans for our pleasure, concubines for our comfort, and wives to give us legitimate children.' No matter what occurred, the woman was always a slave to the man. When she was widowed she became the ward of her eldest son. She could never walk unescorted, and was always guarded by a slave. She never went to the market, as this was a slave's activity. In fact, the Greek term for a wife, in Athenian democracy, was a neutral word that meant 'object whose purpose it is to look after the household.' She was not a person but a thing.*[2] Apart from a few prominent women, and those seen as having oracular powers, the wife's role was restricted. *"When an Athenian bride went to live with her husband she was cut of from her entire family and became a menial worker in her husband's home. She had no rights of her own and functionally was no longer a citizen. She could not vote. The children she bore were not her own. They were the product of male seed, and she was just the container. All the children came from him and belonged to him. A son could only escape his father's authority once he married. The wife was always under her husband's power and always remained secluded in her house".* [3]

The man's father had been widowed, I take it, and had remarried. His second wife, the son's stepmother, would, after the cultural expectations for a new wife, have been a virgin and a relatively young woman, perhaps not far in age from her stepson. Once the father died (much more likely than her being left with the son through divorce) she became the responsibility of her stepson who was now head of the house. Without rights as a citizen or status as a significant family member, and without her own extended family support, she was vulnerable and, in this case, appears to have been used by her stepson, whom Paul holds to be *"the one who did the wrong"* (2 Cor 7.12). The taboos breached by this enforced relationship were strong, making this an unusual form of immorality even in Corinth (1 Cor 5.1). It had to be brought out into the open. One of the reasons, which justify disclosing such private information about another family, may well be that the victim is so under the control of the perpetrator that she cannot speak up for herself. Someone else has to be courageous enough to champion her cause, and to fight her corner. The church is to be the voice of those that have no voice. Certainly she is not censured in any way in the ensuing process.

But, some will say, Paul did not take this matter to the civic authorities; he dealt with it internally in the church corporate, if not totally within the congregation. This is true, but it takes us to the heart of the difficulty in working out our relationship to the civic authorities in any given culture. The issue in question here was not, in that culture, against the law as such, but it did break a strong taboo. There was no legislative code breached, as it did not exist. Advanced civilisations tend to legislate more and more, and so to criminalize more and more behaviours, with associated defined penalties. What would have occurred in Corinth would have been social censure and pressure based on maintaining the family name. The abuse of the weak by the strong, especially in acts of rape or child sexual abuse, is legislated against by our society. These behaviours have thereby been made an official public matter, not just one of private family shame. That means we have the statutory dimension to consider. For us the law of the land has also been broken.

Does that mean that confidentiality should still be retained within the church? Or does it mean that there is a legitimate need to report to the statutory authorities as the servants of God for our good in these things? Does the fact that a sin has become a public crime through legislation rightly bring it under the jurisdiction of the statutory authority as far as God is concerned? The passage in 1 Corinthians 6 does not really help us here, as it seems primarily to refer to civil disputes about financial matters. The lawsuits are *"with one another"* (1 Cor. 6.7), rather than of the Crown -v- John Brown nature. Does that mean that in cases of sexual abuse we should try to keep it in house? After all, the civil magistrates are, in this passage, termed *"those who are least esteemed by the church"* (6.4).

If this passage is taken to mean that the church is to deal **internally** with all criminal matters between those in the church, including the sexual abuse of children, then it exposes the church's failure to deal with these issues historically, for the church, in general, has not had the integrity to do so. I do not believe that such an interpretation is tenable. The issues cannot be buried, treated secretly or 'confidentially', and quiet solutions found that move offenders to other venues where no one knows the risks they pose. The Catholic Church has been severely criticised in the media for just such strategies.[4] On the Protestant side, where all but one of the cases in my experience involving Christian leaders has surfaced, there has not been the same media frenzy, even though the same mentality exists there. We have been too afraid to deal with the issues openly. The failures of the past do not contribute much to our current credibility, though hopefully this is changing. The sexual abuse of children stumbles the little ones and the terms in which Jesus speaks about offenders are so strong that we cannot collude with their desire for secrecy. We do have to deal with such matters as a congregation, but this by no means excludes a second process of criminal investigation pursued by the statutory authorities. Similarly, referral to the statutory authorities does not mean the congregation can wash it's hands of the situation, much as many would want it to.

Consider how Paul directs the church in Corinth to deal with the offender in their congregation, albeit he had offended against another adult. As already shown, the man concerned is identified as the offender or perpetrator. Paul expects and commands that the whole church be the disciplining agent, not just the leadership, or one appointed leader. *"When you are assembled"* (1 Cor. 5.4) he is to be dealt with. There is real importance in this. First secrecy is excluded. Secrecy is not the same as confidentiality. Secrecy is an illegitimate hiddenness, when others should know what has happened, and the brothers and sisters in the congregation here in Corinth needed to know. Some at least already knew what was amiss, as they had blown the whistle to Paul, but everyone needed to know his attitude and what was to be done about it. If this is so when an adult offends against another adult, how much more when he offends against a child?

They were also to be involved in the doing, that is they were not just observers or consumers of the decisions of the leaders as instructed by Paul, though he had already pronounced judgement in the name of the Lord Jesus on the man (1 Cor. 5.3-4). The members of the congregation were told in Paul's letter that the offender was to be excluded by their corporate action. *"Let him who has done this be removed from among you* (5.2). *You are to deliver this man to Satan for the destruction of the flesh . . . . . . "*(5.5)."*Cleanse out the old leaven"* (5.7). *"I wrote to you not to associate with* any one who bears the name of brother if he is guilty of immorality" (5.11). "Drive out the wicked person from among you" (5.13). Five times he commands the offender to be excluded from the privileges of participation in the fellowship. The inertia that makes us shy away from dealing with such offenders is not acceptable, and it is clear that Paul expected each and every member to act in concert. There was to be no hidden support from his friends that would undermine the corporate action being taken. Nowadays we are at an added disadvantage, in that an offender has many other congregations to which he can run without having to suffer the full rigour of church discipline. This raises the issue of inter congregational and interdenominational responsibility to one another in the body of Christ, and will be addressed below.

Paul gives two reasons for the exclusion of the offender. The first is for the man's own sake. It is that *"his spirit may be saved in the day of the Lord Jesus"* (5.5). Somehow, if the congregation takes this action in the right spirit, it will underline the seriousness of the consequences of his sin and may affect him for eventual good, even if this is only realised in eternity. The heart of the action required is redemptive; it is not without hope, albeit it is severe. The second reason is for the health of the remaining members of the congregation. *"Do you not know that a little leaven leavens the whole lump? Cleanse out the old leaven **that you may be a new lump**, as you really are unleavened"* (5.6-7). Not to deal with a matter exposes the congregation to a contamination effect. Undealt with, an issue grows in influence, tenacity and extent. When it is eventually tackled, explanations will have to be given not only for the action at last being taken, but also for the delay, and the latter can be more uncomfortable because the delay is the fault of the church, rather than the offender. The church must take its responsibilities seriously, if it is to be taken seriously, and while we do not wash our dirty linen in public gladly, we show that truth, not expediency, is our rudder.

I believe that the statutory authorities also have a God-given part to play. *"Be subject, for the Lord's sake to every institution ordained for men, whether it be to the emperor as supreme, or to governors as sent by him to punish those who do wrong and to praise those who do right. For it is God's will that by doing right you should put to silence the ignorance of foolish men. Live as free men, yet without using your freedom as a pretext for evil"* (1 Pet 2.13-16). If we collude with offenders through secrecy we dilute our testimony where we live, and create suspicion regarding what we really do together. In a few cases, this sort of internal dealing with abuse has created such suspicion on the part of the statutory authorities, that they have investigated the entire congregation. We must honour the real authority delegated to the state and cooperate with it as far as possible.

The final question in this part is to weigh whether there is a difference in an offence confessed and an offence exposed. If someone comes to confess an offence it is easily assumed that he wishes to change, to be cleansed and to be forgiven. Is that not enough? We may be quite willing to report the offender who is exposed while he is still intent on offending into the future, as he has not willingly come into the light. He has been dragged there kicking and screaming, or at best may be relieved that he now will have to address an issue he had not the motivation to stop himself. It is not common for a child sex abuser to bring his own sin into view; it has however been the case, in my experience, that an offender has been relieved, at least initially, that his offending has been opened up, because his conscience was troubling him even though he had not stopped his abuse. A number of these men withdraw again in some measure when the police become involved and the reality of legal consequences starts to sink in. But the question is whether the duty to report applies in the case where an abuser comes forward to confess and seek help? While it is important to remain supportive to an offender who comes to confess, he is not the only, or even main consideration in the overall picture. The answer to the question is 'Yes', but, if at all possible, in a way that helps the offender retain full responsibility for what he has done, and for seeking the help he needs.

The main person to consider is not the offender; it is the victim who suffered the wrong, often over a lengthy period of time. And secondly, there may be other actual, though unknown, victims, or potential victims also needing protection, who have to be considered, and to whom we have a duty of care. The police will need the written complaint of an adult victim of child sexual abuse, to be able to proceed with a case that can go to court. If this is not forthcoming for whatever reason, the best that can be achieved in our society is some form of child protection action by Social Services in respect of children deemed to be currently at risk from the offender.

Only a small proportion of child sexual abuse cases conclude with an eventual conviction. The victim is still a child and may not want to be exposed to the reliving of the experience in court, as will be necessary if the allegation is denied. The parents, statutory workers involved and the Crown Prosecution Service may feel that the child witness is too vulnerable to be put through the court experience, even with the closed circuit video evidence facility that is now available.

In historical cases, where the victim is now an adult, forensic (blood, semen, saliva) and medical (bruises, tissue damage) evidence will not be available, so the main case will be one word against another. Multiple cases strengthen historical investigations if patterns of offending from the evidence of witnesses unknown to each other can be demonstrated. But even if there is no court case, it is still vital that each situation is investigated as thoroughly as possible to ensure that the maximum help is offered to all alleged victims, and that the full extent of risk posed by an alleged offender is evaluated. This remains true even when, rarely, the offender owns up, and it means that the authorities still have to be involved. It is best if the offender can bring the matter to the police's attention himself, and he should be encouraged to do so in the first instance. This shows genuineness in wanting to change and is the only thing that can give him any credibility. The support of brothers who will stand with him in the process, but who will hold him to the process, can be vital. If he will not do this, there is a duty on those who know to report the man to the authorities without his consent, so that all possible victims can be traced and helped.

Tony, a young man of 26 years, came to see us. He had been sexually abused between the ages of ten and fourteen by an older male. This man had subsequently married into Tony's extended family and had two young sons by the time we met Tony. Tony was deeply stressed by his past abuse and was engaging in some dangerous behaviours as a result. Once he was able to face what had happened to him, and had received some healing in his own life, he was able to start to think beyond himself to the possible implications in the lives of other young men who had also been in the offender's sphere, and to the current risks to the man's two sons. For himself, Tony just wanted to hear the man in question take responsibility for the abuse; at the initial stage he had no intention of going to the police. Without asking our advice and without our knowledge (and against the advice we would have given, if asked) Tony went to the man's minister and told his story. The minister (again unknown to us at the time, and against what we would have advised, had he asked) directly confronted the alleged perpetrator. The man admitted abusing Tony and expressed remorse at having done this. Tony related this to us, asking that I would accompany him to a meeting he had set up with the offender and his minister. He wanted the minister to hold the man to his confession, and me to support him as he had a lot of apprehension in doing this.

When I arrived at the venue for the meeting, the alleged offender and the minister were there already. We afterwards learnt that Tony got as far as the front door, before taking cold feet and leaving, but he did not let us know this at the time. The discussion with the man changed focus slightly as a result, from what he had done to Tony to the more general pattern and extent of his offending. When asked whether there were other victims, he became very uncomfortable and avoided the answer, although it did not take much discernment to read what he was really saying. The question reoccurred in several ways throughout the meeting, until, standing beside our cars when we were leaving, he admitted to me that he thought that there might have been over forty other victims. They had all been young boys at the time, except for one little girl. He explained his involvement with her as having been initiated by her, and he thought that she, because of this, was being abused in her own family. He gave no names or identifying information in relation to any of his victims.

Almost immediately after this Tony discovered that the same man had also sexually abused his younger brother. This revelation decided the issue of going to the police in Tony's mind, a step that he had previously been reluctant to take because of the family relationships that would be disrupted. I tried at length to persuade the perpetrator that the better option for him would be to give himself up, as he would at least be seen as seeking help. In the end he took legal advice and became less forthcoming about his offences. Tony made his complaint to the police, and I also made a statement regarding the information that I had been given by him. The man was arrested, eventually confessing to what he had done, including giving the names of all the victims he could remember. Of those named, twenty-six were able to be located (the offences had taken place over an eighteen year period, and some of the victims could not be traced), and seven of these wished to make a formal statement of complaint. The man was prosecuted and served a term in prison.

His children were placed on the Child Protection Register, though there was no evidence that they had been abused, and on his release the man was not permitted to live with his family, because he did not engage well with the counselling process offered to him. I do not know the current situation, as we are no longer involved. The point is that, without a full police investigation, many hidden victims would have been left without any sense of redress or offer of help. Now, in their own time, they can seek the help they may need without the pressure of being witnesses in a pending court case. To deal with the offender in isolation, as the confessional does, is a limited but inadequate response to the whole entangled picture. Confession has, in many cases, to lead to restitution of some sort, even if this is just to take the responsibility back to where it belongs. Once it becomes public through the proper means, the door is opened to restoration and healing at many levels for all the victims.

Notes.

1. See, for example, Adams, J.E., "The Christian Counsellor's Manual", Presbyterian and Reformed Publishing Company, 1973, p15; Yoder, J.H., "The Politics of Jesus", W.B Eerdmans, 1972, chapter 10; Compendium of the Social Doctrine of the Church, Librerai Editrice Vaticana, Burns and Owens, 2004, paragraph 393.

2. Breiner, Sander J., "Slaughter of the Innocents", Plenum Press, New York and London, 1990, p47.

3. Ibid. P46

4. Cashman, H., "Christianity and Child Sexual Abuse", SPCK, 1993, see pp 62-66 for details for many such cases.

Chapter Ten

Restoration of an Offender

Every investigation and conviction will have consequences for an offender, and the process he has to walk through will affect the timing of the issues that face the local congregation. While taking account of the legal processes, this section is about the responsibilities of the fellowship that has to deal with him also. All discipline is to be restorative rather than punitive and that is what we now must consider.

There are two sides to what must happen if a perpetrator is to be restored successfully. There is the perpetrator's responsibility to deal with himself, and there is the responsibility of the congregation to deal with him, and to be in the place where they can deal with him. The child sex offender has stumbled a child, or *"caused a child to sin"* (Matt 18.6). But this is not the only type of stumbling that Jesus points out in the passage. He refers to a man stumbling himself by misuse of his own hand, foot or eye. Logically this internal stumbling must precede him stumbling a child. It is at the deeper, internal level that he must, according to Jesus, deal with himself, lest he incur the most serious of consequences.

As Jesus puts it, the man must cut off hand or foot, or pluck out his eye, if those are the means of him stumbling himself. He is to do this to himself; no other person can do this for him, whatever else they may have to do to him. It is his own personal responsibility to be ruthless in dealing with his inclination to sin against a child. According to Jesus, the man's eternal destiny depends on whether he does this work or not. The consequence of dealing with his issues properly is that he can *"enter life".* That this means eternal life, rather than society, is clear by comparison to the consequences of failing to deal with himself this thoroughly. Failure results in him being *"thrown into the eternal fire"* or *"thrown into the hell of fire"* (Matt 18.8,9). The seriousness of this requirement, laid down by Jesus himself, cannot be over stated. God will not be mocked by shallowness or pretence. The man's repentance must be real or it will in the end be found out. The other side of the coin is the responsibility of the local church.

In the experience of Paul it was neither automatic nor easy for the church in Corinth to fully, openly and thoroughly address the issues with the family there, and our contemporary experience matches this. The prospect of restoring any sex offender, but especially a child sex offender, within the congregation where his sin occurred and was addressed, is even more daunting, for us as much as for the church in Corinth. Paul does not seem to have been deterred by the fact that this was a young church, with a raw leadership team at best, if indeed a leadership team had yet been established. He does not seem to have been deterred by the fact that many of the members had been involved in a wide range of sexual sins before coming to faith in Christ (1 Cor 6.9-11), and that some of them were still dabbling in their previous sexual life patterns (why otherwise does he have to warn them against prostitution, for example? (see 6.15-20). He does not even seem to take into account that the congregation is split into several parties which are at loggerheads with each other, vying for position and control, though he has already addressed this issue earlier in the letter. He requires them to grow up in responsibility forthwith, though they do not even understand what love is, and he has to explain even this to them (1 Cor 13). It appears that he will not wait until they are of sufficient stature, by most of the yardsticks that we might wish to use, to face this challenge. But, amazingly, he uses this extreme situation to require united action from them all, both in relation to the discipline of this offender, and in respect of the more general sexual laxity and lack of true love in the fellowship. He sees the situation as an opportunity to take vital ground in their personal and corporate lives, to grow up in learning what love actually is! That is faith in action.

Yet Paul is aware that what is involved here is a long process, with stages, until the final goal is achieved. This is what we have to explore now. The idea of restoration is suspect to many professionals working in this field. The reasons for this include the fact that no one talks in terms of a 'cure', and there is a growing awareness that what we now call sexual orientation is not readily accessible to simple processes of change. Barriers or taboos, once breached in one's self, are difficult to rebuild, some would say impossible. If that is so, the corporate management of the individual, to ensure the protection of the children concerned, should be more our focus than the search for a wonder pill or therapy. That does not mean that therapy is of no value. Where it rebuilds inhibitions towards children and illicit sexual activity, where it brings awareness of the impact of abusive behaviour and its associated emotional manipulations of the victim, and where it engenders a willingness to be 'policed' by one's brothers as a price of being accepted, then it is of real value. This is true whether intervention greatly shifts the individual's basic orientation and desires or not.

Further, the question is not whether or not we should accept such individuals back into a congregation. We have to realise that these offenders, whether convicted or not, are in many congregations, whether we know it or not, and we cannot wish them away. Paul, dealing with this adult sex offender, does not avoid the long-term journey for the man himself or for the congregation.

When Paul writes his second letter to the Corinthians about one year after the first, we get an insight into their reaction, over that period, to the instructions in the first letter. It seems that he had wanted to visit again between times (2 Cor 1.15-2.1), and it appears that Titus had in fact visited on his behalf (7.13-16). However, the time lapse between the two letters is significant as it shows that their response was not transitory but sustained. *"For even if I made you sorry with my letter, I do not regret it (though I did regret it), for I see that that letter grieved you, though only for a while. As it is, I rejoice, not because you were grieved, but because you were grieved into repenting*

Child Sexual Abuse and the Local Church

......*For see what earnestness this godly grief has produced in you, what eagerness to clear yourselves, what indignation, what alarm, what longing, what zeal, what punishment! At every point you have proved yourselves guiltless in the matter"* (2 Cor 7.8-9,11). The next sentence, referring to the victim and the perpetrator, establishes that he is indeed dealing again with their biggest pastoral mess.

There had been seriousness and intensity in the way the church had worked through the teaching of the first letter. I take this to include the teaching on sexual relationships and marriage, all of which was related to the main issues in the central case. They could not have dealt with the sex offender without also looking at all the related areas of their own lives highlighted in the process. The whole church was in the process of cleaning up their lives to live in sexual purity, and to represent Christ's covenant relationship with the church in their marriages. This was not accomplished in a few seminars; it took a good year of continued focus before Paul, who obviously kept himself well briefed, could instruct them to start the restoration process. It had always been the desired best outcome, though at the outset it was not clear how things might go; now, a year later, they had to shift in their response to the offender, and they were in a better place themselves to do this.

Some have understood this in such a way as to derive a rule of thumb that a man should be relieved of public responsibility for a period of a year before consideration of restoration to ministry. I do not think that the time span in this case should be seen as normative in this way. The issue is whether or not he has repented, should it take him six months or five years. Of course it may well be that a minimum period for standing down is wiser, rather than a hasty restoration to public ministry. However, it needs to be underlined that the man in Corinth does not seem to have carried any public responsibility, and the issue to be decided was simply his re-inclusion in the fellowship. The moral failure of a leader may therefore warrant a significantly longer period before participation in the fellowship and restoration to public ministry can be considered, and if he has offended against a child he may never be able to resume in any leadership role again.

They could not have reintegrated the offender, even if he had substantially changed, unless they themselves had walked an equally tough journey to be able to do so. For the church at Corinth the timing of the step to initiate restoration is gauged from outside, and prompted from outside. There will not easily be the motivation from within the congregation to effect reconciliation. On the other hand, there is no other alternative offered to the offender regarding where he might be restored. In his home congregation he is known, the risks are known, responsibility is accepted and they are to seek to work it all out together. This is also a big ask for us, especially in a culture that wants solutions immediately and does not like risk.

In Corinth it reaches the point when the *"punishment by the majority is enough"* (2 Cor 2.6). Yes, he has caused pain to everyone, but the objective of the exclusion of the offender from the congregation has, we infer from the instruction given, been attained. He has repented and is now in danger of excessive sorrow (2.7). Paul could not have encouraged restoration unless he was convinced that repentance was deep on the offender's part. But he also felt that the progress made by the faithfulness of the congregation in general was at a point where they could cope with the reintroduction of the man back into their midst. If the man's stepmother was an ongoing member of the fellowship, the other people there would have been more able to keep some awareness of his progress as she could have provided the best reference for any changes apparent in his life. If she was not a member of the fellowship, this would not apply.

Paul asks that now they *"should rather turn to forgive and comfort him, or he may be overwhelmed by excessive sorrow"* (2.7). He begs them to reaffirm their love for him (2.8). This is not duty speaking but real love that desires a gracious outcome for everyone. They were not asked to forgive the man a year earlier; that would have been premature. Signs and fruit of repentance are required before forgiveness can be pronounced, though no doubt the church had prayed much for him. They actually express forgiveness at the point at which the offender is in a fit state to be received back into fellowship. This reinforces the discussion in chapter eight above. The church cannot, any more than the victim, be hurried into pronouncing forgiveness before they have completed the journey in themselves to be able to do so. Neither can it happen before the offender has truly repented and wants to be accepted back. The fact that they are told to **turn** to forgive him underlines that as a body their back (metaphorically) has been towards him over the intervening period of a year, in line with Paul's initial instructions on how to deal with him. Paul knows that it is painful for them to obey; he himself felt the pain acutely, but he loved them enough to hold them to the tough path they have to walk (2.1-5).

The church is again given reasons why they must now restore the offender. The first is for his sake. His punishment of exclusion is enough when it has served to bring the offender to true repentance; that is, it is restorative, not punitive. He needs to be accepted, forgiven and comforted lest he is overwhelmed. He will also be much safer towards others if he is surrounded by those who are committed to him on the basis of truth. Secondly there is an imperative to forgive for the sake of the church itself. They are to forgive for their own good. Paul, assured that the man has repented, has already forgiven him for the good of the church. *"What I have forgiven ...... has been for your sake in the presence of Christ, to keep Satan from gaining the advantage over us; for we are not ignorant of his designs"* (2.10-11). There is a supernatural dimension to restorative forgiveness. The man was delivered to Satan for the destruction of the flesh (1 Cor 5.5), now he is to be restored to fellowship lest unforgiveness opens the door to Satan gaining an advantage over the church. Sin has to be dealt with, but when dealt with restoratively, it has to be forgiven to lock the door against Satan. Lack of repentance on his part, or lack of forgiveness from the community of the forgiven, opens the door to demonic intrusion and disruption. The church cannot afford to short-circuit or avoid the process, for the sake of its own health, and perhaps survival.

It is worth noting that Paul describes the discipline exercised on this man as being by **the majority** (2 Cor. 2.6). This implies that there was not total consensus in the church at Corinth with the steps taken. Perhaps it is unrealistic to expect that every single person will be able to pull together in standing with the discipline. However it is for the ultimate benefit of the church that the majority hold firm. Why did a minority not go with the instruction of Paul in his first letter? What happened them as individuals? We are not told, but my experience has been that some of those, who disagree with how an individual is dealt with in such a difficult case, leave the church and go elsewhere. There was no 'elsewhere' in Corinth. It is possible that some at least remained in the fellowship in Corinth for, in spite of the progress of the body of the church, Paul is concerned at the end of his second letter to them, that when he comes eventually to see them that *"my God may humble me before you, and I may have to mourn over many of those who have sinned before and have not repented of the impurity, immorality and licentiousness which they have practiced"* (2 Cor. 12.21). Perhaps this is further evidence that when we do not deal with issues in our own lives by the word of God, we cannot be in the place to redemptively deal with others who have sinned.

The whole sequence as recorded in both letters does not go into detail regarding how the offender came to repentance, or how the victim, his stepmother, was healed. The two letters are written to the church regarding how **the church** should walk out these issues in its common life. *"This is why I wrote, that I might test **you** and know whether you are obedient in everything"* (2 Cor 2.9)… *"So although I wrote to you, it was (not on account of offender or victim, but) in order that **your** zeal for us might be revealed to **you** in the sight of God"* (7.12). God allowed the whole event, though it tarnished his name in their midst. Thankfully, he is not proud, rather patient, not willing that any should perish. He calls us up to a way of living that requires us to really know him if we are to walk it out. We can settle for less, believing the task is hopeless, but we settle for disobedience and satanic interference if we do. Such an event challenges our understanding and experience of the grace of God to the core. Are we willing to walk out discipleship and obedience together and be radically changed in the process in areas where we already thought we were above the line? Are we not the Corinthian church in many ways? There is so much sexual sin imported from the past and still nurtured in our hearts that we are no longer surprised when a leader falls, let alone a member of the body. Have we made friends with these enemies to such an extent that it will take a public crisis for us to humble ourselves and let the word of God do its work in us? God is prepared to go that far to get us clean. Lord, teach us to fear you, as we ought!

It is interesting to note that unlike the first letter there is very little teaching in the second letter to the Corinthians on love, marriage and sexuality related issues. We are told not to be unequally yoked with an unbeliever (2 Cor 6.14), which is often rightly applied to marriage to someone who is not a Christian. Apart from that, the last reference is at the end of chapter twelve where Paul clearly still had concerns about how deeply some of them had responded in their hearts. These issues are hard to shift, but they never become acceptable to God or to his servant. They show that thoughts, like those of Eve, have been led astray, by the serpent who deceives, from a sincere devotion to Christ, to whom we were presented as a pure bride to her one husband (11.1-3). This is a spiritual battle centring on the temptations that appeal to our human sexuality, even within the body of Christ. Thankfully there is The One who goes after strays, and the possibility that we each can be like him if we so choose.

Am I my Brother's Keeper?

Again, there are two sides to this question, one within the local congregation, and the other between congregations in the body of Christ. We have seen enough of the experience of the young congregation in Corinth to know that Paul certainly wanted them to be the keepers of their erring brother. That responsibility would tax them deeply and include self-reflection and change of life-style. It took them several years to outwork the entire process and we do not know whether they all managed to fully achieve this. With the high profile of child sexual abuse issues in our society, it is helpful to consider how practically these things can be processed most effectively.

Paul addressed the issues in Corinth in writing. Any subsequent verbal exchanges would have been in the context created by his letter to them. In the letter, the requirements on the church were held in permanent form; in fact we still have them for our own instruction. This writing down is very useful as it enables the writer to objectify the main points and set them down together, and it enables the recipients to hold in mind the range of things they are being committed to do. It is easy, if matters are only verbal, to hear the one statement that impacts each of us the most, and to miss the fine print and subsidiary points if we depend on hearing alone.

We work with churches that have a child sex offender in the congregation. We help them to collate the basic information they need to understand the nature of the risks this person brings. Only then can the church devise the full range of support strategies for the offender, and the full range of protective strategies for all the children that are needed. We encourage the development of a small group to be placed around the offender, sometimes called a 'circle of support'. We identify someone who, with the co-operation of the offender, will seek to obtain, from the authorities, full and accurate information about the number and nature of the offences committed, and the terms of the sex offender risk management plan that the statutory authorities have put in place. This sort of partnership can be beneficial for both the church and the professionals involved, if both sides can get beyond suspicion and mutual distrust. The fellowship's risk management plan is shared, preferably devised, with the offender, and what is expected of him is clearly outlined. He must know the insecurity his presence causes, and accept that he has to be accountable to enjoy the privilege of belonging. The price of belonging is openness and brokenness. If he finds this unacceptable he may move elsewhere, but this congregation at least is safe, and the leaders will have done everything that they could. If he accepts these limitations and stays, maximum protection is put in place and the church fulfils its duty of care to all the children and families in the sphere of its activities. No leadership team gains credibility by vague, or semi-secret plans and ideas of how to manage such a situation, especially if the offender re-offends. If the worst should happen, the leadership will want to be seen to have done everything in their power and to have tried to prevent any reoccurrence.

If an offender decides to move from one congregation to another, the responsibility of the leadership team does not end there. We believe that there is a duty of care to other congregations, and, in particular, to any other congregation to which he may go. Our experience is that offenders who move are not doing so because of the style of service, the ethos of the fellowship, or the doctrinal position of the denomination or church fellowship. They move to what they perceive is a place where they are not known, or where they will be accepted without any rigorous monitoring or 'intrusive' support. They are likely to cross denominational boundaries in an attempt to find a network of people unrelated to the one they have just left. This calls for grace throughout the body of Christ, including towards other churches with whom we may disagree substantially, even on basic truths.

The more an offender is prepared to move around, the more the whole body of Christ, and society in general, should be concerned. The multi-disciplinary team of professionals, who have drawn up the official risk management plan for the individual, will be likely to take on the responsibility for informing a new congregation of the presence of a child sex offender. However, this team is unlikely to understand the range of Biblical responsibilities, which a church leadership should be motivated to put in place. The sharing of information between congregations becomes a vital child protection strategy, and should therefore be written in the congregation's risk management plan from the outset. The offender then has agreed to this, or at least knows what will be done, if he moves. This situation is analogous to the apostolic warnings in the New Testament in respect of false brethren, deceivers, and false apostles, that is, men who may do serious harm (2 Cor 11.12-15; Gal 2.4-5; 2 Tim 4.14-15). Individuals, who have committed offences against children, may not all be false brethren, but they do constitute a serious risk, which will have to be monitored. Once aware, the receiving congregation picks up the responsibility to follow through the process of discipline and restoration from whatever point it has reached. This may include encouraging reconciliation with the home fellowship at some point.

Child Sexual Abuse and the Gospel

We have been involved in just such situations with the 'donor' and 'receiver' churches in the same case. In one case, the church of origin had applied church discipline, and put some other measures in place to deal with the emerging problem in the congregation. The offender and his extended family left the church in protest and surfaced in another congregation of another denomination in a neighbouring town. The leader of the church of origin advised his counterpart in the second congregation, who decided to receive the family. No carry-over discipline was exercised, effectively undermining the actions of the church of origin. Only when the leader in the second congregation left several years later did the wider leadership team feel in a position to address the situation. This was considerably more difficult because the offender had become used to a degree of acceptance in the fellowship. Putting in place a risk management plan retrospectively was very uncomfortable for both him and the church. In the heart of the situation the question of ongoing risk to children was not seriously discussed until the leader in the second church had departed. This loss of focus, for whatever reason and however well intentioned, increases risk to children and is a failure in our duty of care. We need to accept that we are in these situations for the long haul, and we need to plan and review accordingly. If we can, the experience of exercising long-term responsibility will grow us as people, as disciples, as churches and, God willing, in the end we will not be fazed by whatever comes our way. We are called to be faithful and to endure. How will we respond when God gives us the learning opportunity?

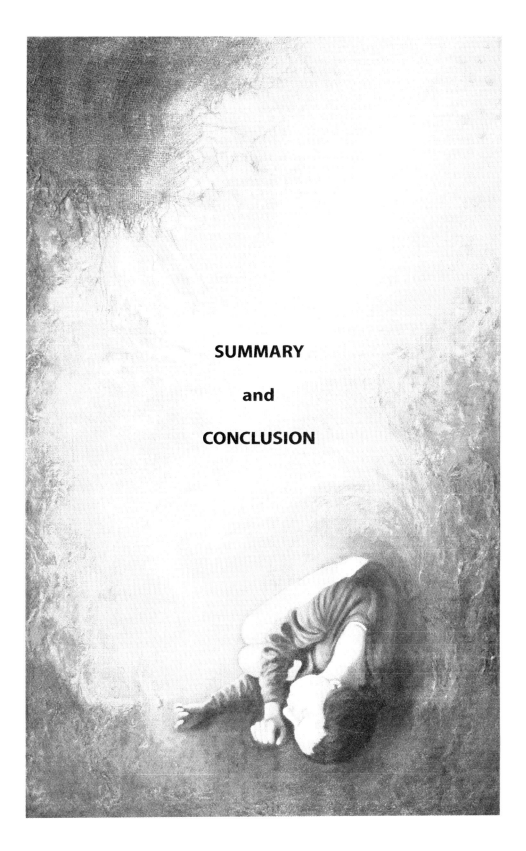

SUMMARY

and

CONCLUSION

Summary and Conclusion

The purpose of this book has been to construct the Biblical material dealing with child sexual abuse and related issues into a relevant format for those who are in church leadership, and may find themselves responsible for managing a complicated situation with little or no warning. To be equipped to work such problems effectively, leaders and those involved in pastoral care need to understand the dynamics of child sexual abuse in families from the perspectives of the perpetrator, the victim, and the range of stances that can be adopted by those who are entangled by family or friendship ties with the two main people involved. They also need to have a grasp of how the Gospel applies to the many and various ways that specific struggles manifest in the lives of the respective individuals involved, and be willing to help them find God's perspective, and his ways of escape for them. It is vital for leaders to be aware of how their Biblical responsibilities to the parties interplay with the legal and statutory circumstances in our country. This includes how they should manage the initial crisis of realisation, the resultant fallout, their responsibilities to their congregation, other congregations, in some circumstances, and to society in general. This is above and beyond their commitment to the main parties involved.

How do we conclude? If we take Jesus and his word seriously, there are a number of things that become imperative. The way we treat children reflects and reveals the way in which we treat Christ himself. If that is so, the church, which has so often shovelled the abuse of children under the carpet, has been guilty of colluding with the abuse of Christ. We need to repent and become the champion and protector of "the little ones", **and** "our brother's keeper". This means affirming fatherhood in every possible constructive way, alongside the demonstrating of the unique value of every child. It requires a willingness to take on responsibility and to act restoratively towards those who come to faith with a history of abusing or having been abused, without jeopardising one while we seek to assist the other. It means holding to account those from within the ranks of the church who have abused children, and requiring openness and brokenness from them as the price of ongoing belonging, even as we believe that they can still be restored. It means providing a place of safety for the children in our churches, and addressing the currents in our society that war against children. It means learning to minister to those who were abused as children and who carry the scars.

Malachi says we are to *"turn the hearts of the fathers to the children"* and then *"turn the hearts of the children to the fathers".* The loss of effective fatherhood in our culture is reaching epidemic proportions, but it remains the God-given target for change that will affect the destiny of our nation. The establishment and encouragement of 'colonies' of people where family is being restored and issues addressed is no small task, but the church has to become more like what she is meant to be. We can model restoration of family, reconciliation in relationships, love of the brothers, being our brothers' keepers, and respect for children, men and women, if we are willing to pay the price. John the Baptist, as a single man, did it in his generation, at great personal cost. We must do it now in this generation, as parents, members of the body of Christ and citizens, and leave a deposit for future generations in the process. This is the heart of our God for us and for our children. *"And he will come to Zion as Redeemer, to those in Jacob who turn from transgression, says the Lord. And as for me, this is my covenant with them, says the Lord: my spirit which is upon you, and my words which I have put in your mouth, shall not depart out of your mouth, or out of the mouth of your children, or out of the mouth of your children's children, says the Lord, from this time forth and for evermore" (Is 59.21).*

Child Sexual Abuse and The Church
Appendix 1 ~ Simon Bass - CCPAS
Principal safeguarding legislation across the United Kingdom

Safeguarding legislation across the United Kingdom is very similar, having at its core the U.N. Convention on the Rights of the Child. To assist the reader the following may be helpful in placing the context of the book within the specified legislative framework for each constituent part of the UK. For example the Children Act 1989 and 2004 sets the legal framework for children's welfare and protection in England and Wales. In Northern Ireland it is the Children (Northern Ireland) Order 1995 and in Scotland the Children (Scotland) Act 1995. All these laws share the same principles and they are all subject to the Human Rights Act 1998 and the United Nations Convention on the Rights of the Child (UNCRC).

The UNCRC defines a child as:
"A child means every human being below the age of eighteen years, unless, under the law applicable to the child, majority is attained earlier." [Article 1 – Convention on the Rights of the Child, adopted by the UN in 1989 and ratified by the UK in 1991].

Whilst there is different legislation and government guidance throughout the UK setting out the duties and responsibilities of agencies and organisations to keep children safe, they all agree with the UNCRC definition that a child is anyone under the age of 18.

Though safeguarding legislation throughout the UK contains the same principles and ideals it is helpful to look at the specific requirements, as they affect churches and other places of worship where working with children and young people.

Churches can help protect children from harm in three ways:
- having clear policies and procedures in place to promote the welfare of children and in responding appropriately to concerns,
- in the safe recruitment and supervision of those working with children and young people whether in a paid or voluntary capacity, and
- in providing a safe environment through having in place guidelines and boundaries especially with those who in the past have harmed those who are vulnerable.

The legislation that follows covers these aspects of safeguarding in our churches.

England Legal Framework

The principle safeguarding legislation in England setting out the legal framework for children's welfare and protection comes from the Children Act 1989 and the Children Act 2004. The Children Act 1989 places a dual obligation on Local

Authorities with regard to children. Local Authorities have a duty to promote the welfare of children in a general sense and also to safeguard children from harm.

The Children Act 2004 and the accompanying Every Child Matters: Change for Children (2004) 'staying safe' programme, places a duty on services to ensure that every child, whatever the background or circumstances, to have the support they need to:
- be healthy
- stay safe
- enjoy and achieve through learning
- make a positive contribution to society
- achieve economic well-being.

The Children Act 2004 also established Local Safeguarding Children Boards (LSCBs) for each Local Authority area. LSCBs provide an inter-agency forum capable of a strategic and tactical input into the delivery of services for children. Places of worship should be represented on LSCBs either within the full board or as part of any sub groups. LSCB's produce safeguarding policies for all agencies in their area based on 'Working Together to Safeguard Children – A guide to inter-agency working to safeguard and promote the welfare of children,' which is statutory Government guidance issued in 2006.

'Working Together' as its name suggests, emphasises the importance of an integrated approach towards protecting children, with different agencies involved with children cooperating with each other and sharing information in order to protect children from harm. The guidance specifically addresses faith communities (within Sections 2.152 to 2.155) recognising the work undertaken by churches with children. The guidance states that places of worship should have procedures for safe recruitment, appropriate codes of practice for staff and know where to seek advice on safeguarding issues.

All those working with children should be safely recruited including application forms, interviews and references in line with Safe from Harm (1993) recommendations issued by the Home Office for voluntary organisations. In addition a Criminal Records Bureau (CRB) disclosure check should be undertaken, which provides information about an individual's criminal background. For those working with children it is possible to have an enhanced disclosure, which contains the following information:
- Police National Computer (PNC), including Convictions, Cautions, Reprimands and Warnings etc.
- Lists maintained by the Independent Safeguarding Authority (ISA);
- Non-conviction information held by local police forces.

Disclosure checks are available through registered or umbrella bodies with the CRB.

Child Sexual Abuse and The Church

The Independent Safeguarding Authority (ISA) has been created to help prevent unsuitable people from working with children and vulnerable adults. It does this by placing these people on one of two ISA Barred Lists. The ISA makes decisions about who should be on these lists as part of the Vetting and Barring Scheme (VBS). The VBS Scheme deals with activities that are classified as 'regulated' or 'controlled'. These activities include both paid and unpaid (voluntary) work.

The ISA began operating in October 2009. From November 2010 it will be a legal requirement for individuals to register with the ISA if they intend to work or currently work with children and/or vulnerable adults in England, Wales and Northern Ireland. There is a five-year phasing for the entire workforce of those working with children and vulnerable adults.

Sexual and violent offenders worship within our churches, as this book shows. It is therefore essential that places of worship liase with the statutory authorities to ensure adequate risk assessments are carried out where an offender wishes to be part of any faith community. Some offenders will come under MAPPA - Multi Agency Public Protection Arrangements. These are the statutory arrangements for managing sexual and violent offenders. The Responsible Authority (RA) charged with ensuring that MAPPA is established in an area consists of the Police, Prison and Probation Services, though all other agencies including places of worship have a responsibility to co-operate with the RA. Section 6.5 of Version 3 of the MAPPA guidance (2009) the guidance covers 'Offenders and Worship' and shows how RAs should assist religious communities to put in place effective arrangements' which allows them to protect their community whilst allowing the offender to maintain their right to worship but in a safe way. It states that places of worship and religious leaders should be provided with sufficient information to protect their congregation. As well as signposting who to contact within the faith communities the guidance also advocates that offenders agree to and sign an undertaking of behaviour.

Wales Legal Framework

The principle safeguarding legislation in Wales setting out the legal framework for children's welfare and protection comes from the Children Act 1989 and the Children Act 2004. The Children Act 1989 places a dual obligation on Local Authorities with regard to children. Local Authorities have a duty to promote the welfare of children in a general sense and also to safeguard children from harm.

The Children Act 2004 and the accompanying 'Rights in Action' programme, places a duty on children's services authorities in Wales to ensure arrangements are made to improve the well-being of children in the authority's area relating to:
- physical and mental health and emotional well-being;
- protection from harm and neglect;
- education, training and recreation;

- the contribution made by them to society;
- social and economic well-being.

The Welsh Assembly Government (WAG) has adopted Seven Core Aims through which it works to ensure that all children and young people:
- Have a flying start in life;
- Have a comprehensive range of education and learning opportunities;
- Enjoy the best possible health and are free from abuse, victimisation and exploitation;
- Have access to play, leisure, sporting and cultural activities;
- Are listened to, treated with respect, and have their race and cultural identity recognised;
- Have a safe home and a community which supports physical and emotional well-being; and
- Are not disadvantaged by poverty.

The Welsh Assembly Government issued 'Safeguarding Children - Working Together under the Children Act 2004' (2007), emphasises the importance of an integrated approach towards protecting children, with different agencies involved with children cooperating with each other and sharing information in order to protect children from harm. The guidance specifically addresses faith communities (within Sections 3.56 to 3.59) recognising the work undertaken by churches with children. The guidance states that places of worship should have procedures for safe recruitment, appropriate codes of practice for staff and know where to seek advice on safeguarding issues.

Additionally the 'All Wales Child Protection Procedures' (2008) are an essential part of the wider agenda of safeguarding children and promoting their welfare. The common standards they provide guide and inform child protection practice in each of the 22 Local Safeguarding Children Boards across Wales. They outline the framework for determining how individual child protection referrals, actions and plans are made and carried out.

The Children Act 2004 also established Local Safeguarding Children Boards (LSCBs) for each Local Authority area. LSCBs provide an inter-agency forum capable of a strategic and tactical input into the delivery of services for children. Places of worship should be represented on LSCBs either within the full board or as part of any sub groups.

All those working with children should be safely recruited including application forms, interviews and references in line with Safe from Harm: Safeguarding Children in Voluntary and Community Organisations in Wales, (2008) recommendations issued by the WAG. In addition a Criminal Records Bureau (CRB) disclosure check should be undertaken, which provides information about an individual's criminal

background. For those working with children it is possible to have an enhanced disclosure, which contains the following information:
- Police National Computer (PNC), including Convictions, Cautions, Reprimands and Warnings etc.
- Lists maintained by the Independent Safeguarding Authority (ISA);
- Non conviction information held by local police forces.

Disclosure checks are available through registered or umbrella bodies with the CRB.

The Independent Safeguarding Authority (ISA) has been created to help prevent unsuitable people from working with children and vulnerable adults. It does this by placing these people on one of two ISA Barred Lists. The ISA makes decisions about who should be on these lists as part of the Vetting and Barring Scheme (VBS). The VBS Scheme deals with activities that are classified as 'regulated' or 'controlled'. These activities include both paid and unpaid (voluntary) work.

The ISA began operating in October 2009. From November 2010 it will be a legal requirement for individuals to register with the ISA if they intend to work or currently work with children and/or vulnerable adults in England, Wales and Northern Ireland. There is a five-year phasing for the entire workforce of those working with children and vulnerable adults.

Sexual and violent offenders worship within our churches, as this book shows. It is therefore essential that places of worship liase with the statutory authorities to ensure adequate risk assessments are carried out where an offender wishes to be part of any faith community. Some offenders will come under MAPPA - Multi Agency Public Protection Arrangements. These are the statutory arrangements for managing sexual and violent offenders. The Responsible Authority (RA) charged with ensuring that MAPPA is established in an area consists of the Police, Prison and Probation Services; though all other agencies including places of worship have a responsibility to co-operate with the RA. Section 6.5 of Version 3 of the MAPPA guidance (2009) the guidance covers 'Offenders and Worship' and shows how RAs should assist religious communities to put in place effective arrangements' which allows them to protect their community whilst allowing the offender to maintain their right to worship but in a safe way. It states that places of worship and religious leaders should be provided with sufficient information to protect their congregation. As well as signposting who to contact within the faith communities the guidance also advocates that offenders agree to and sign an undertaking of behaviour.

Scotland Legal Framework

The principle piece of legislation for child protection in Scotland is the Children (Scotland) Act 1995. This sets the legal framework for children's welfare and protection in Scotland. The Act places a dual obligation on Local Authorities with regard to children. Local Authorities have a duty both to promote the welfare of children in a general sense and also to safeguard children from harm. The intention of this legislation is to ensure that all the welfare and developmental needs of children are met, including the need to be protected from harm.

In Scotland, Children's Hearings deal with children and young people under 16 (in some cases under 18) who commit offences or are in need of protection. At the case conference a decision will be made whether to make a referral to the Children's Reporter. A Children's Hearing is made up of three panel members (known as the Children's Panel). The Hearing discusses the circumstances of the child fully with the parents, child or young person and any representatives. The Hearing is concerned with the wider picture and long-term well being of the child. Any decisions will be based on the best interests and welfare of the child.

The Scottish executive published a guide to inter-agency co-operation 'Protecting Children – A Shared Responsibility' in 2000. This publication set out a framework for inter-agency collaboration between Social Work Departments and other agencies; the document defines the various types of abuse and outlines arrangements for responding to particular cases of suspected abuse or neglect. Following on from this they launched 'Protecting Children and Young People: The Charter, and Protecting Children and Young People: The Framework for Standards' in 2004. The Children's Charter consists of 13 statements from which the Framework for Standards was developed.

The eight headline standards:
- Standard 1: Children get the help they need when they need it;
- Standard 2: Professionals take timely and effective action to protect children;
- Standard 3: Professionals ensure children are listened to and respected;
- Standard 4: Agencies and professionals share information about children where this is necessary to protect them;
- Standard 5: Agencies and professionals work together to assess needs and risks and develop effective plans;
- Standard 6: Professionals are competent and confident;
- Standard 7: Agencies work in partnership with members of the community to protect children;
- Standard 8: Agencies, individually and collectively, demonstrate leadership and accountability for their work and its effectiveness.

All those working with children should be safely recruited including application forms, interviews and references in line with 'Protecting Children – A Code of Practice for Voluntary organisations in Scotland' (1995) recommendations. In addition a Scottish Criminal Records Office (SCRO) Disclosure Scotland check should be undertaken, which provides information about an individual's criminal

background. For those working with children it is possible to have an enhanced disclosure, which contains the following information:
- Police National Computer (PNC), including Convictions, Cautions, Reprimands and Warnings etc.
- Till 2010: lists maintained under the Protection of Children (Scotland) Act 2003 known as the Disqualified from Working with Children list.
- From 2010: lists maintained under the Protecting Vulnerable Groups Scheme (PVG Scheme)
- Non conviction information held by local police forces.

The Protecting Vulnerable Groups Scheme (PVG Scheme) has been created to help prevent unsuitable people from working with children and vulnerable adults. It does this by placing these people on one of two PVG Scheme Barred Lists. The Scheme will go live in 2010.

Sexual and violent offenders worship within our churches, as this book shows. It is therefore essential that places of worship liase with the statutory authorities to ensure adequate risk assessments are carried out where an offender wishes to be part of any faith community. The Management of Offenders (Scotland) Act 2005 requires the police, local authorities and the Scottish Prison Service (known as 'Responsible Authorities') to jointly establish arrangements for the assessment and management of risk posed by sex offenders and violent offenders. This is undertaken in Scotland through Multi Agency Public Protection Arrangements (MAPPAs).

Northern Ireland Legal Framework

The principle safeguarding legislation in Northern Ireland setting out the legal framework for children's welfare and protection comes from the Children (Northern Ireland) Order 2005. The Order places a dual obligation on Health and Social Services Board with regard to children. They have a duty to promote the welfare of children in a general sense and also to safeguard children from harm.

To assist with this 'Co-operating to Safeguard Children' was issued by the Department of Health, Social Services and Public Safety (DHSSPS) (2003). The document outlines how Area Child Protection Committees can develop strategies, policies and procedures to safeguard children who are assessed to be at risk of significant harm.

All those working with children should be safely recruited including application forms, interviews and references in line with 'Our Duty to Care' recommendations for voluntary organisations. In addition an Access Northern Ireland (Access NI) Disclosure Service check should be undertaken, which provides information about an individual's criminal background. For those working with children it is possible to have an enhanced disclosure, which contains the following information:

- PSNI Computer, including Convictions, Cautions, Reprimands and Warnings etc.
- lists maintained by the Independent Safeguarding Authority (ISA);
- non conviction information held by local police forces.

Disclosure checks are available through registered or umbrella bodies with AccessNI.

Under the Safeguarding Vulnerable Groups (Northern Ireland) Order 2007 a church can ascertain a person's suitability for working with children or vulnerable adults through the Independent Safeguarding Authority (ISA). The ISA makes decisions about who should be on these lists as part of the Vetting and Barring Scheme (VBS). The VBS Scheme deals with activities that are classified as 'regulated' or 'controlled'. These activities include both paid and unpaid (voluntary) work.

The ISA began operating in October 2009. From November 2010 it will be a legal requirement for individuals to register with the ISA if they intend to work or currently work with children and/or vulnerable adults in England, Wales and Northern Ireland. There is a five year phasing for the entire workforce of those working with children and vulnerable adults.

Sexual and violent offenders worship within our churches, as this book shows. It is therefore essential that places of worship liase with the statutory authorities to ensure adequate risk assessments are carried out where an offender wishes to be part of any faith community. The Northern Ireland Office has produced the Public Protection Arrangements Northern Ireland (PPANI) in 2008. These build on the Multi Agency Sex Offender Risk Assessment and Management (MASRAM) procedures, and are statutory and require agencies to share information and work together to manage the risk posed by both sex offenders and certain violent offenders. This guidance states that churches should be informed where they have responsibility or control over the offender and other persons who may be at risk from the offender.

Appendix 2
About CCPAS and Family Spectrum Limited

CCPAS

The Churches' Child Protection Advisory Service (CCPAS) is the only independent Christian charity providing professional advice, support, training and resources in all areas of safeguarding children and for those affected by abuse.

Our services are used not only by churches and groups across the denominational spectrum, but increasingly by other faiths as well as non-faith based organisations keen to utilise the resources and expertise we offer. We also give advice to Children's Services Departments, Police and other agencies across the UK.

CCPAS provides a 24 hour telephone helpline (0845 120 4550), act as an umbrella body for disclosure checks throughout the UK and have resources, available from www.ccpas.co.uk

FAMILY SPECTRUM

The ministry of Family Spectrum was established in early 2004 to respond to the many and varied complexities in family related issues, which are increasingly arising in local church/fellowship life. The founder, Willie Patterson, had worked for over 30 years in Causeway Health and Social Services Trust, and was Assistant Director for Family and Child Care when he resigned to set up Family Spectrum. He had for many years been regularly asked by church leaders to advise on, and with his wife, Hazel, to become involved in complex family related situations on behalf of congregations. These included the full range of child abuse and protection issues addressed in this book, human sexuality related issues, marriage breakdown and divorce issues, and disrupted and reconstituted families. The goal of the ministry is to support the development of leaders on the ground in their capacity to address and manage these issues Biblically.

Family Spectrum can be contacted for copies of this book, or in relation to any of the issues above, at info@familyspectrum.org.uk or by telephone at 02870353057. Further information can be found on the web site at www.familyspectrum.org.uk.

Family Spectrum can be contacted at info@familyspectrum.org.uk